THE COMEBACK

I have known Dave Scatchard now for almost two decades. I still have yet to see Dave have a negative attitude toward anything in his life. Now I'm sure he has his days and his problems like everyone else, but he has an amazing ability to put the positive spin up front and personal for all to see. Always willing to help a friend or a stranger is one of his best qualities. Laughter comes easy to him—whether saying something funny or being the first and loudest laugh at another's attempt to be funny.

A glass half full doesn't represent Dave one bit. The glass is overflowing! It takes a strong person to deal with and aid other people's problems, issues, or emotions, but Dave leaps at the opportunity. Not for his financial benefit but for the personal satisfaction to know he's made an impact in another life! They broke the mold when they made Dave. The world, especially now, needs more people like him! The ability to reinvent himself the way he has is not easy for an ex-professional athlete, but Dave has done it multiple times. This quality to never accept failure or be denied in life again is a God-given gift. I trust him with my life and my secrets and know that they are both safe forever. He's a guy I know I will call my friend as long as I'm walking above ground.

—Jeremy Roenick, nine-time NHL All-Star
and two-time Olympian

Dave and I met as twenty-year-old rookies in the NHL and became roommates and best friends for two years. Dave was, from day one, somebody you wanted to be around, as he always had great energy and a positive attitude. He has been through a lot, but I know regardless of what path life takes him on, he will find a way to be successful and continue to be the person who everyone wants to have in their life. Dave, I'm proud to call you my friend.

—Mattias Ohlund, NHL Star

As a kid, hockey player, and adult, Dave has held a secret to success. He's a doer, directed by a strong moral compass and fueled by a positive-action attitude. It is an attitude that seeks self-improvement. It has taken him to the heights of success and most importantly continues to guide him through life's obstacles. It is an attitude that is contagious and inspiring.

—Jason Potter, life-long friend

Scatchy is a super nice guy, and I'm honored to call him my friend! He always treats everybody with the utmost respect. Dave is extremely competitive, and in my personal experiences with him, he approaches new challenges with a thirst for success that cannot be quenched! But what makes Scatchy so special and so unique is his extreme positivity! Dave will find a way to shed positive light onto everybody and every situation, no matter how bleak things might appear!

—Greg Mueller, three-time World Series
of Poker Bracelet Champion

I am so proud of our hockey family and how each player who has ever played the game at the highest level conducts himself and represents our sport with such integrity. Every teammate who has ever played with Dave Scatchard loves his intensity, competitive spirit, and team loyalty. As I've gotten to know him as a person, I enjoy his humor, joy of life, and love of family and friends. I hope you enjoy his story of dedication and inspiration.

—Bryan Trottier, Hockey Hall of Fame Inductee 1997

THE
COMEBACK

MY JOURNEY THROUGH
HEAVEN AND HELL

DAVE SCATCHARD

LIONCREST
PUBLISHING

THE COMEBACK
My Journey through Heaven and Hell

ISBN 978-1-5445-1515-1 *Hardcover*
      978-1-5445-1513-7 *Paperback*
      978-1-5445-1514-4 *Ebook*

This book is dedicated to my dad, a man who allowed me to chase my dreams fearlessly, and who I always knew believed in me. A man with the wisdom of someone who had a direct connection to the truth; a man who would help anyone, anytime, because that was the fabric that he was made of. He was my hero, my friend, and my idol.

I love you, Dad. I miss you, and I hope you're having fun in heaven.

P.S. Give God a hug for me.

CONTENTS

INTRODUCTION

It takes a lot to make a hockey player quit.

The MCL tear in Milwaukee didn't do it. Neither did the second MCL tear in St. Louis. Concussions are part of the game, so not even the first...second...or third...could really get my attention. I semi-retired after the fourth but found my way to some miracle treatments that got me back on the ice. Even after the fifth concussion took my memory, my focus, sometimes even my will to live, I still felt the pull to keep playing. A million bucks to play in Russia made me think hard about coming back. Tax-free money, big ice surface, less hitting—I could make that work.

Looking back on it now, I realize there are times in your life when God tries to help you move on to the next phase. As it turns out, he'll go pretty far to get your attention. But when hockey's all you've ever done, it's hard to hear those messages. What else was I going to do? The comeback was what I knew. I got knocked down over and over again, and I always figured out a way to get back up. For every setback, there was a comeback. I did it my entire life, so why should this be any different?

I always got better. I always pressed on. I always had hockey.

But the Mayo Clinic's battery of tests was telling me I had to figure something else out. My family was telling me I had to figure something else out. My body was screaming at me to give it a break. But all I was thinking about was whether I could trick the tests, ride out whatever was going on in my head, and get back out to play.

Sitting in the doctor's office after months of failed tests and lack of progress, he pulled 3D MRI results up on his computer and tried to explain what was actually happening in my brain.

Why I had debilitating headaches.

Why I couldn't be out in the sun or inside under bright lights.

Why I couldn't find the right words.

Why I couldn't take a simple shopping list to the grocery store—or even remember why I was there.

Why the computer of my brain was running on an ancient dial-up connection that seemed to always have static on the line.

Why I felt like a shell of a man.

Why there was no way I could shrug this off like every other injury.

I nodded along while he pointed to the images and talked about how the concussions had shoved my brain into the front part of my skull like a screwdriver. He told me there was scar tissue and shearing where connections should have been.

Instead of pathways from A to B, my thoughts had to detour around, something like A to Z to M before finally coming back to B. That's why I was slurring my speech, had no memory, and always seemed to have to search for answers.

That's why I needed to quit hockey.

But I already knew that.

God had already told me—in person.

I just wasn't ready to listen.

///

There's not a great way to describe what happened to me during the last injury of my hockey career. Later in the book, you'll see that part of my story begin:

I remember the puck dropping at center ice. I remember skating forward fast with it on my backhand. I remember pitch black like someone turned out the lights, then floating up, looking down on my crumpled body on the ice as the paramedics and my trainer worked on me...

What came after that I'll only ever be able to convey in bits and pieces. How do you explain something that we don't have words for? I'm going to try because I promised God I would. But I could write a hundred books and never come close to describing what actually happened.

There was no big, booming voice telling me what to do. In fact, there was nothing tangible at all to hang onto. It was a place of weightlessness, love, and joy—the most beautiful feelings I'd ever felt in my life. I was more relaxed, happy, and free than I had ever been before in my life. It was pure ecstasy—enough that I felt torn about whether I should wake up.

No, not wake up. Leave. I wasn't asleep. I was in a very real, incredible place, and I had a choice to make. Just one—I had to get back to my family. I would have done anything for another chance at life with them. So after an honest conversation that was difficult to have, I made a promise, a commitment with the love and light that surrounded me—a deal with God that I would come back to share both this incredible love that I had felt and my story. The light would fade. The weight and pain would return. But my family would be waiting for me.

My promise to God was simple and difficult: just share all that unconditional, radiating love that I felt in God's presence with every soul that I came into contact with. Tell my story and watch what happened.

I tried to explain to the paramedics what I had seen as soon as I opened my eyes, but my jaw was a mess, and I couldn't get the words out. I didn't know it just then, but I would struggle with words and thoughts for a long time to come. I had more to discover and more to learn before I could find healing and share it with the world. But it was the journey I was given. The path I'm still walking to this day.

This book is the most complete record of my story, years after I made my promise. And it's been burning inside me this whole time.

///

I'll be honest, there were times when I questioned whether I made the right decision to come back.

I was happy to be home with my family, but as half the man I used to be, was I really doing them any good? My pain wouldn't go away. My memory wasn't coming back. I felt stupid when I talked to people, so I avoided everyone. Most of my days were spent hiding by myself in the dark, and a lot of nights, I drank myself to sleep for the hope of a little bit of rest. I lay in bed thinking over and over, "Is this really what I came back for?"

It takes a whole lot to make a hockey player quit, but taking everything away from him will get you pretty damn close. In fact, at times I was ready to do anything it took to get away from the pain and suffering that I was in. My mind would play tricks on me and try to convince me that suicide was the only way to make it all go away. To get back to that light and love. To take away the pain for good.

When I share my story now, I can see it resonating with people who have experienced trauma. With fellow athletes, with soldiers and firefighters, with police officers and first responders—our modern-day warriors and gladiators who have had to become someone else to do things that they never imagined doing. I see you, man. I understand better than most that nobody teaches you how to go back and forth between normal life and trauma. All I know is it's too heavy to carry on your own. That weight will crush you.

I believe in my heart that we've only got so much personal energy to use in a day, and if we have to use up large pieces of it just trying to survive, trying not to be scared, trying to heal, and attempting to get our shit together, it makes it difficult to get anything else done. We just run out of energy after we are done managing our day-to-day lives. We're giving everything we have to this beast that our circumstances sat on our shoulders.

That weight is what the brain injuries felt like for me—like something that had been dropped onto my shoulders, and I had to figure out how to move on with life while dragging that monster along with me. At first, I thought I needed to destroy it. If I wasn't going to end my life, maybe I could put the pain in the closet and pretend it wasn't there. Bury it like I had done with everything else in my life and keep going until I could function enough to fake it. If I could get back to playing hockey, I was sure I'd never see that monster again. Forget how mangled my body and brain were. I just needed to get back on the ice.

The thing is, my wife already wanted me to quit. My parents wanted me to quit. And now I could barely function, and my doctor had flat out told me I had to quit. I'd pushed them all off by another game or another season or another deal for years already. It's the hockey player's mentality. Pretend you're not hurt and just keep going. I even called up my buddy Patrick Fisher to talk to him about what it would take to get onto the ice one more time.

Fishy had been one of the first players Wayne Gretzky brought onto the Phoenix team I played on, and we'd both arrived in Phoenix pretty close to the same time. After some years battling bad habits and things about his life that he wanted to change, Fishy went back to Switzerland to start coaching. When I called him, he had just gotten back from living with a shaman in the jungle in Peru for an extended period of time. He was glad to hear from me, but instead of talking about playing on his team in Switzerland like I'd hoped, the conversation took a very different turn. He could see past my bullshit, and he was so tuned in after his trip that he almost started prophesying over me right there on the call. Like God was talking right through him.

He said, "You know, Dave, I think you're not really seeing what's going on here."

I was scared to hear what he might say next, probably because I knew what was coming. He continued anyway:

"Here's the deal. God's been trying to tell you to stop it. You're done. Yeah, you get your fourth concussion and get away with it. You're a little off balance, but a year and a half later you see the other side and decide to make a comeback. You're an overachiever and want to do things your way, so you try out as a walk-on for the Canucks but don't make the team. That's another message that you're done, but Nashville offers you a two-way deal, and you take it.

"You play amazing, but they screw you over. Your wife's at home with babies, and you're leaving her behind. Then you blow your knee out. When Nashville doesn't give you the deal you deserve, you keep forcing it instead of listening. So you go to St. Louis, and they screw you over too, and then you blow your knee out again. You still haven't listened.

"Then God comes in with a thunderclap, knocks you out cold, and has a long conversation with you to tell you *in person* that it's over. And you're calling me to say you want to play again? Are you fucking kidding me?

"You've had a great career. It was a great run. You made money, did things you've always dreamed of—but buddy, there's more to life than hockey. It's over."

He was right. I knew it. I was done. I was broken. I was empty. And I had to figure out what was coming next.

///

It took a long time to figure out how to live in freedom here on earth, but everything I needed was right there in me and around me, waiting for me to find it. I had to learn that losing hockey wasn't the same as losing my life, and even though it was dark, light could still be found. Even though I had all that pain to deal with, the incredible love and light that I experienced had come back with me. All of the grace and freedom, joy and bliss, gratitude and love never left me. Maybe I had it all along.

Just like it's in and around all of us.

And that was the deal I made with God. I just had to take all that love with me and spread it around to as many people as possible. That was it.

The key was to stop shoving my pain into a closet or trying to destroy it. We can't turn that part of ourselves off any more than we can live like a blissed-out monk, disconnected from everyone and everything. The warrior who helped us survive this long? That part still has a place. It's still honored and loved for what it helped us do. And the monk has a place too. The dad and the husband and the son in me, the writer and the hockey player, the coach and the coached—they all have a role to play. Even the fighter, the bullied, the injured, the wrecked and dead and alive again but barely hanging on. All of it. It's all part of the light and love and peace that's right here on this earth.

This is my story. These are my successes and victories. My broken body and shattered mind. My healing and my comeback.

This is my love and my light and my breath and my life.

And I haven't quit yet.

CHAPTER ONE

HOCKEY IN A COAL TOWN

X

N o one ever really taught any of us kids how to skate. In the tiny town of Hinton, where I grew up, it was just something you did.

When I talk about those days now, my friends here in Phoenix don't get it. But the brutal winters up in Hinton, Alberta, freeze the ice so deep that you can actually drive out onto the ponds and lakes. The adults could even circle up their pickup trucks and drop their tailgates to barbecue. Sometimes the ice was thick enough to have a small campfire on it, too, if you can believe it.

From the time I was two or three years old, my parents would strap these tiny skates to my feet and let me shuffle around on the ice. When I was really little, I would push a chair around the ice to keep my balance. None of us could afford a net, so someone would set boots out as the "goal." Little kids would just fool around with the pucks and work on their stick handling and moves. Bigger kids would sink the pucks into snowbanks when they'd score, and we'd have to dig them out to keep playing.

There was something magical about it, especially when the snow kept falling. All of our dads would shovel the surface clear, and we'd skate. No lessons, no techniques. Just the ice.

My dad looked forward to those weekends just as much or more than we kids did. He started off as a PE teacher when I was really little but then decided he could take care of us better if he worked in the coal mines. The weeks were long, but he couldn't wait to take us out there once he was off. That's what we did, almost every weekend, all winter long. Hockey was more than a game. It was part of my childhood—who I was.

///

By five years old, I wanted to sign up to play hockey for real. I daydreamed about hockey. I drew pictures of jerseys and hockey sticks. I decided that's what I wanted to be when I grew up. I watched every game that I could, and I prayed every night that I could get a real net and one day make it to the NHL. My dad surprised me with one for Christmas and set up in the basement at first. That became my new playtime, just shooting the few pucks I had, over and over again. I started off all over the place, leaving holes in the wall where I missed and sent pucks through the drywall. If my dad cared, he didn't show it. He just smiled, fixed the holes, and suggested moving the net outside.[1] *Game on.*

Every single night, I'd stay outside playing street hockey with my net and a ball, mimicking my idols, taking on anyone from the neighborhood who wanted to play, like a pretend Wayne Gretzky. That incredible '80s-era Oilers team was mine. When dad got the occasional pair of tickets through work, we'd jump in the car and drive the three hours down to Edmonton and back the same night, even if I had school the next day. We couldn't afford a hotel, but tickets are tickets. You go when you can.

A kid couldn't ask for a better group of guys to grow up watching. Wayne Gretzky, Mark Messier, Glenn Anderson, Grant Fuhr, Andy Moog, Kevin Lowe. And then they won *four Stanley Cups in five years*. It was a true dynasty, and I was so blessed to be able to cheer on such an amazing team.

My street hockey games ran nightly, as long as we weren't off to a real game, with pucks or tennis balls and two boots as the second goal, just like I'd learned from toddlerhood. The only problem was scoring on the boots side meant running forever to get the ball or puck back. So when someone else in the neighborhood finally got a second net, it was like Christmas for all of us.

---

1   I probably shot ten thousand pucks into that net. I used it for ten years until one day I shot a puck right into the middle of the bar, and it finally cracked and broke. I thought it was the best investment my dad ever made.

A few other kids would filter out to join me until they had to go in for dinner. Then another set of kids would come out to play until it got dark out. At some point, my parents would tell me I had to eat or I wouldn't be allowed to play anymore, and I'd be forced to come in and heat up dinner. If I could, I'd go back out again after that, even if it was cold or snowing or dark, and even if I was the only one.

At first, we split the seven or so kids who lived in the neighborhood into teams. The older I got, the more I practiced, and eventually I could play against everybody at once. I'd run around playing defense and offense with no goalie, loving every second of the challenge. As soon as my little brother got big enough to sit in the net, I made him some pads out of old couch cushions and laces. I put a catcher's mask and glove on him and cut a blocker out of cardboard. Then we could *really* take them on.

This is how hockey started for me. It's how my life started—with so much support and opportunities to play that even the hardest days didn't feel like work. I was doing what I loved, surrounded by people who loved me. I was a little ball of joy and light.

And I do mean *little*.

///

Yeah, I was a skinny kid. It was embarrassing, really. Especially for a kid who wanted to play in the NHL one day. Maybe racing home from school every day and telling my mom "just one more game" for hours and hours had something to do with why I couldn't gain any weight. I was strong and fast, but for years I was one of the smaller kids on the ice.

My dad gently mentioned it to me once when I said I wanted to go pro. He said, "You know, I think hockey players have strong legs." Instead of discouraging me, he was planting a seed. He went on, "What do you think you could do to make your legs stronger?"

That's how he always talked to me about the NHL. Questions like "What do you think you'd have to do to improve enough to make it?" and "What can you do here at home to get better or stronger?" These quality questions taught me how to go after my dreams. Later on in my life, whenever I couldn't quite figure something out, I would go back to this method. I would ask better questions about what it was going to take, or what I was going to have to commit to in order to achieve whatever I was going after.

I decided to shoot a hundred pucks a day—which, first of all, meant I needed more pucks. At seven years old, I only had a few bucks in allowance to my name, but I knew where to get them. When we'd watch the older players practice and play at the local rink, they would sometimes shoot pucks off the cross-bar and over the glass. And when that happened, I could run to find them and put them in my pockets to take home and add to my milk-bucket collection. My collection grew until it only took one rotation through the bucket to hit my goal for the day, and my dad held me to it.

Once, it was snowing so hard outside that I could barely find the pucks after I shot them. My dad didn't force me to stay out there—he just asked me how bad I wanted it. So I put on my boots and gloves and toque and showed him. That day, I shot more like three hundred pucks—every single one of them felt like I was getting further and further ahead of the kids who didn't want it bad enough to practice on their own in a blizzard.

When he asked me what I needed to do to get my legs stronger, I decided to ask Santa for ankle weights. On another happy Christmas morning, I was thrilled to find a ten-pound box under the tree. I put the weights on right then, with my pajamas still on, and kept them on for breakfast, all day, and even bedtime. I didn't really take them off for years. They fit great on top of these brand new, amazing skates with in-line wheels that my dad and I discovered a few years later.

We first saw them at a one-man street show where a guy reenacted the Canada Cup. There were maybe twenty people in his whole audience, and me and my dad were his biggest fans. I loved the show, and I especially loved what he was skating around on. They looked like blades that didn't need ice. When we talked to him afterward, he told my dad about the one store in Canada where you could get them on backorder. By then I had a paper route, and I saved up all of my money to order one of the earliest pairs of Rollerblades ever made. With my ankle weights strapped to the top, I didn't take them off for years.

I did my paper route in them with my giant bag of newspapers strapped to my back. I played street hockey in them. I skated the three or four miles to school in them. And one day, when all the kids in my neighborhood were loading up into the bus, I skated up and pointed at the driver. *You and me. Let's go.*

I took off as fast as I could. He passed me up right away and got an early lead, but soon he had to get more kids. As he pulled to a stop, I pulled away, jumping off the curbs and back onto the sidewalk, racing as fast as I could go. When he caught back up, the kids had their arms sticking out the window, yelling and cheering.

This became my morning and afternoon commute. Every single day, four miles there and back. I was training hard, without even realizing what I was doing. My skinny little legs were building up a tolerance, and my great big heart was falling in love with the work ethic that would define my career.

With all of the work I was doing, my parents didn't feel like they needed to send me to camps when I was a kid. Not until things got serious later on. It felt like hockey was my life, but there were so many other parts of our world to love, too.

Our summers were spent in a cabin out in British Columbia for as many weekends as possible. That's where my dad taught us how to wakeboard and barefoot water ski. Me and my younger brother and sister spent our summers making slingshots, scuba diving, running around the lake, and dirt biking through the trails—stopping short with a bull moose on the trail or stepping outside to see bears hanging out in the trees.

The year I got a Sony Discman, I had to figure out how to go running without the CD skipping every ten steps. I decided to hold it out flat like a waiter serving a dish while I ran my heart out through the trails of BC. I looked ridiculous, but it worked... sort of.

Oh, and I did beat the bus to school. Eventually, it wasn't even close anymore.

///

Back then, hard work didn't feel like work. Everything became a new way to train, get stronger, and get better. That kind of work ethic definitely came from my dad, from how he talked to me about hockey to how I watched him live his life.

I always wanted to be like my dad. I still do.

When he picked up work at the coal mines, he took night shifts and spent a lot of his days with us. After practice or games, he'd go to work. Sometimes he'd pick up a day shift and go right to a game. I'm honestly not sure when he slept. The smell of coal on his clothes and skin was a constant reminder of how hard he worked to take care of us.

There wasn't anything he couldn't do. He had all of us water skiing from the time we were little kids. He was one of the first hang gliders in Canada. He was a total MacGyver who could fix anything—and often would, even for people we passed who had broken down on the side of the road. He never wanted anything in return. He just loved life and took care of people.

My dad wasn't overly affectionate, but we knew he loved us. He was strict but fair. My mom wasn't a disciplinarian like he was. She was the source of endless love and support in my life. Where my dad sacrificed hours of work for us, she stopped working to raise us kids. They were the perfect yin and yang for me. What my dad couldn't give me, she could, and it worked the other way around too.

My mom often reminds me that she's the one who drove me to the arena and signed me up for my first skating lessons and hockey team. And she's right—she should get that credit, especially since so many of my early stories are about my dad. He used his PE experience to be my hockey coach almost every year through my entire minor hockey career.

He was an amazing coach. I was progressing quickly enough that they let me play with the kids who were two years older than me. Pretty soon, our team outpaced the league, and we got kicked out for being too far ahead of the other kids. We were beating teams 17-0 or 20-0. It wasn't fun for their kids, so they wouldn't play us anymore. That didn't stop my dad. He learned how to drive a bus and called around Alberta to get us exhibition games. Sometimes we drove hours to get a game.

I was ten or eleven before I realized I might actually have a future in hockey.

We were on our way to a game in Edmonton, which usually meant some kind of practice rink on the outskirts of town. Instead of pulling off toward one of those smaller venues, Dad kept driving into the heart of Edmonton. As he pulled up to the Northlands Coliseum—the Oilers' stadium—he told us, "All right, guys. You're playing where the big boys play tonight."

I still don't know how he pulled it off, but it was amazing. We drove in under the stadium and took the players' entrance. I was too excited to wait, so I got fully dressed, gear and all, a full thirty minutes before it was time to take the ice. Banners and logos for the Oilers were all over the place. A few players were around, working out or just hanging out. And when I finally got to take the ice, a couple of teammates and I skated right to the logo in the center and kissed the ice. Our idols skated there. Our best nights ever happened right in those seats—though the nosebleed section looked way higher from my vantage point on the ice than it seemed when dad and I cheered down from it.

Only our parents and the parents from the other team were in the stands that night, but I could almost hear a full crowd roaring for us. For me. I knew I wanted to come back one day to play in a real NHL game.[2] And it actually felt like things were getting serious.

After a peewee game, an older bantam player I loved came down to referee for us to get some extra ice time. Jason Myrel. After the game, he actually skated up to me and asked for my autograph. "I want to be the first one to have it," he told me, and we exchanged signatures for each other. Around the same time, a scout named Barry McLarity started showing up to more and more of my practices. Slowly but surely, my hard work was starting to pay off.

A year or two later, Barry's interest turned into an invitation to a junior camp for St. Albert—my first one. Dad was hesitant. It was just a developmental opportunity, and with the fees plus travel and hotel, it was probably just a cash grab for the junior team. Cash we didn't have.

He must have seen the disappointment on my face, but I didn't complain. I knew my parents sacrificed a lot just for me to play, so I told him I understood and left it at that.

A couple of days later, he came back to me with a solution: "If you don't mind sleeping in the Suburban, I think we can do it."

Don't mind? I was ecstatic! I thanked him a dozen times, tackled him with a hug, and promised to give it everything I had.

"I know you will." He smiled. "You always do."

---

2   My first NHL game against the Oilers, in that same stadium, was so surreal. I skated around, looking up at the full stands and feeling all of the hope that ten-year-old me had felt…and then I saw one of my old teammates' dad! I flicked a puck from center ice over the glass toward him, and he caught it out of the air. It could've been right out of a movie.

A few weeks later, he and I loaded up my gear and our sleeping bags into his red Jeep Suburban—a work truck that was fairly worn down from years in and out of the coal mines. Three hours later, we pulled into St. Albert and found an all-you-can-eat buffet-style restaurant. I did eat all I could, and on my second trip to the ice cream station, my dad laughed about how much energy I would have the next day if I kept piling up the calories. Really, I would need them for staying warm that night.

Outside of the rink in the lot where the camp would take place, we folded the backseats of the Jeep down to make room for our makeshift beds. I was rail-thin, all long and skinny, and between the cold and my excited bundle of nerves, I couldn't stop shivering long enough to sleep. Sometime around three, Dad zipped our sleeping bags together, and we started to warm up, but then I started to worry about registration opening a few hours later, and...it was one of the coldest, longest nights of my life. While the prairie winds ripped through the cracks and seams of my dad's old mining truck, I pictured the ice, the scouts, the other players, and how I might do until eventually I passed out from exhaustion.

I woke up to the sound of car doors slamming and only felt groggy for a second. All of that pent-up energy came bursting out of me as I woke my dad up, threw on shoes and gloves and my jacket, and braved the icy wind to get my hockey bag and sticks from the back of the truck. I paused for a moment when I spotted a fully bearded, older teenager walking in with gear over his shoulder. Maybe there were two sheets of ice, and he'd be skating on the other one—because he was definitely outside of my twelve-to-fifteen age bracket.

Then we spotted another guy, this one with muscle lines you could see through his jeans. And he had equipment too.

Inside, the freezing hockey arena felt warm compared to the night before, but it was the players who had my attention. Those big, bearded dudes were in the same registration line I was in. I felt like a young sapling standing among a bunch of oak trees. Even more surprising, the registration table had my name down, right next to all of theirs. None of us could figure out why. That camp was for sixteen- to twenty-year-olds, and when they asked how old I was, I squeaked out that I was twelve. I stood there wide-eyed and waiting while my dad talked to the GM and tried to figure out how we could salvage the drive and freezing cold night.

"Do you really want to play?"

I looked up at both my dad and the GM. Though the GM was more reluctant about it, they were leaving it up to me.

"They're big and tough and mean. They're going to fight, and it's going to be a lot rougher and more physical hockey than you're used to. We just don't want you to get hurt. Do you really want to play?"

My dad already knew my answer, I think, but he looked into my watery eyes when he asked—probably trying to figure out if those were tears from disappointment or fear. It was probably both. The guys around me were at least twice my size and could really hurt me, but we'd driven all that way and spent the night in the cold. Something inside of me that was louder than the fear told me to do it, and a voice braver than what I felt said, "Let's do it."

My dad waived the team's responsibility for my safety. A man with gray hair and a St. Albert Saints jacket told me they would keep a close eye on me, and I headed down the tunnel to get dressed to skate.

The guys in the locker room were just as surprised to see me as I had been to see them. There were some snide comments tossed my way, but a guy with a hairy chest let me sit next to him as I slid on my Cooperall long pants, grabbed my full-cage face mask, and waited for the coach to give us his speech.

"You represent the best players from around the country, and everyone here is looking for something special. Do what makes you stand out. If you're a fighter, fight. If you're a scorer, score. If you're a goalie, stop the puck. Go do what we brought you here for."

I couldn't have stood out more if I tried. I was the only one in Cooperalls, which had apparently gone out of style for the older players by then. Everyone else had half masks with visors and tall socks with short hockey pants. I was an awkward, gangly spruce among redwoods, wearing goofy equipment that made me look even skinner than I was.

While we were warming up the goalie, in a semi-circle above the circles, my teammates' slap shots hit the ice like thunder. My slap shot clinked off of my stick and slid so slowly the goalie didn't even care to look at it.[3] I'll never forget that first shift of camp, either. The second the puck dropped, the wingers next to me both dropped their gloves and started fighting. My jaw dropped as I looked away from them trading punches, over to the guy across from me who clearly wanted to fight too, and

---

3   To be fair, it did slide into the net while he faced the shooter two down from me. The teammates who saw this were doubled over laughing.

then over to my dad in the stands. He was a little tense but just rolled his eyes. I wanted to scream, *I'm twelve, dude!* and I bet my dad wanted to, too.

Somehow, I survived the first period. By the second, I made a few decent passes and started to relax a little. In the third, I took a shot that hit the goal post. My agility was saving me, and I started to realize my skill set was better than some of the players out there. Now I had the attention of the scouts—and a plan to get some new hockey pants and socks of my own.

I hopped in the shower and made plans to cut my Cooperall pants off in the Jeep that night, not really paying attention to the guys around me. I did overhear something about bald eagles, which seemed strange. I hadn't ever seen one, but I figured they must live in that area. I finished showering and got dressed and then realized there were more guys talking about bald eagles—and now they were laughing. The stories got more and more outrageous, at least to them. I didn't get any of it, and it didn't matter. I was just proud be that much younger and out of place while still kind of holding my own on the ice.

My dad was waiting for me when I walked out of tunnel, beaming and so proud of me for surviving. I thought he might know if there were bald eagles around since all the guys were talking about seeing one earlier in the day.

After a brief moment of confusion, he smiled again and asked if I happened to be in the shower earlier in the day.

I was twelve. It was me. I was the bald eagle. *That's why* it had been so funny.

Unfortunately, the plan to cut my Cooperall pants off went awry, and I misjudged the length by an inch or two. The next day, I didn't look any more like I belonged than I had that first morning, and I was still the bald eagle. But hey, at least I had a nickname of some kind, and I did feel better playing.

That night, we ran into an old friend of my dad's who offered us a place to crash. I accepted before my dad could say no, and my skinny body finally enjoyed a warm night of sleep. The last day of camp, I strutted into the dressing room feeling proud and almost like I was supposed to be there.

The guy playing center across from me didn't agree. The wingers didn't seem to be up for intervening, so it was me and him. Without any way out, this bigger player began trying to intimidate me and slash me. He kept coming after me, knowing that I couldn't do anything about it. Each time he caught the back of my legs or my wrists with another slash, I would wince and vow to get even. Halfway through the first period, I spotted my opportunity.

He was skating up looking backward for a pass, and I sped up as I read the play. The puck came to him, and while he kept his head down, I picked my speed up. With perfect timing, I slammed into him and ran him over. He was completely unaware of what had hit him. I kept my speed up as my defenseman forwarded me the puck that the hit knocked loose, and in one move I ripped a shot high to the glove side of the goal.

I jumped up and down, and my teammates swallowed me up in a hug—the guy I ran over was getting up off the ice, and he was pissed. I had to keep an eye out for him the rest of the game, but I didn't go up against him again until about three minutes left in the last period. The game was tied, 3–3, and a slash that glanced across the back of my legs told me he was back. I pretended not to hear him as he yelled, "Do you wanna go, you little puke?" and I skated as fast as I could toward the goal.

My defenseman again hit my tape with a perfect pass, and the speed I'd picked up skating for my life meant I was alone and once again facing the goalie. Without any time to think, I whipped out a forehand-backhand move and watched the puck hit the back of the net as I ripped it between the goalie's pads.

This time, instead of just celebrating, I turned to brace for the sucker punch I knew was coming. Instead of hitting me, he missed and caught the tough guy on my team who had wrapped me up in a bear hug. Inside, I cheered my tough guy on as he stopped hugging me and turned his attention to the guy who had been chasing me and fed that kid his lunch.

It was one of the only times I skated away from a fight, but I think everyone understood.

My dad grinned from ear to ear all the way home.

///

After that summer, the scouts kept calling and tracking my progress. But when my dad took a job with the highways department out in British Columbia the year I turned thirteen, they lost track of me. I almost lost track of myself.

Leaving Hinton was more bitter than sweet. My dad and I were the first to go to our new town—Salmon Arm, BC, where we already had the summer cabin. It wasn't as fun in the winter, but at least it wasn't as brutally cold as it could be in Alberta. That's how he got the job that took us to BC in the first place. A guy with a highway department told him, "If you ever want to get out of that snow, I've got a job for you." And we definitely wanted to get out of that snow. Dad's only concern was whether I would lose my hockey opportunities if we left Alberta. In the end, he figured if they wanted me bad enough, they'd find me.

Moving out to the cabin in the middle of the winter was boring, to say the least.

Without the lake and the trails and the summer fun, all the lack of amenities in our cabin—no TV, no running hot water—were much more noticeable. I didn't even have my siblings to play with, since they stayed back with Mom in Alberta to sell the house. That process took months and months and put all kinds of stress on the family until it was done.

Dad would go to work at five or six in the morning, so I'd go with him and do homework until it was time for school. I stayed a little after school was over until he could come get me after work, and then we headed back out to the cabin.

Once, when our PE class was learning rugby, a bigger, awkward kid, turned around in front of me and accidentally elbowed me right in the mouth. Blood started pouring out of the hole in my mouth immediately, and I was in total agony. The teacher pulled me into the nurse's office, and they started making calls to my dad at work.

No answer.

I sat there swapping out soggy napkins and letting the blood from my smashed tooth and gums drip into a plastic cup while they kept trying to call my dad to get me to the dentist.

Four hours later, he got off the highways and was finally reachable. The dentist tried to save my tooth, but it didn't work. It eventually turned gray and later needed a root canal—my first dental casualty, and it wasn't even due to hockey.

The tooth bothered me not for what it felt like or looked like but because it was a symptom of something bigger. I was sad and lonely out there during that first year. It was just me, my dad, the radio, and our matching alto saxophones.[4] I missed my mom. I missed my little brother and sister. I missed my team—and I missed being challenged.

The team in Salmon Arm wouldn't let me play up with older players like I had for so long. Plus, the coaches were nice enough, but they weren't my dad. I was taking a serious step backward, and it showed up in my habits. Because I could score at will, I stopped working like I needed to back when I was playing with the big kids. I could slack off and still get by.

That was the last year my dad let another parent coach me.

The next year, we settled into a new house and got my net back up again. I shot in the rain, the heat, the snow, the rain. I was there until the sun went down and I couldn't see where the pucks were going, and I moved beyond a hundred pucks a day to set bigger challenges for myself. I'd have to shoot it off the bottom left post ten times before I could go in for dinner or into the top right corner twenty times before I could stop. I'd have to hit the same spot twenty-five times in a row, starting the count over any time I missed.

With that fire back inside of me, the scouts found me again, just like dad hoped they would. Three years after moving to Salmon Arm, we were playing the provincial championship.

---

4 Yep. I was in the school's jazz band, and my dad knew how to play too. When you're living in a summer cabin in the winter, you find ways to entertain yourself. Playing saxophone with my dad was just as good a thing as any. Maybe better than most.

The whole town showed up to pack shoulder to shoulder into our little arena, standing room only, and a broadcast on the local TV station. We went into triple overtime in the final game of the provincial tournament, and then we won, just like we'd envisioned at the beginning of the season. It felt incredible.

Something had already changed. A shift was coming, and I could never go back.

And as far as I could tell just then, I was ready.

CHAPTER TWO

A KID ON HIS OWN

✕

he scouting inquiries kept coming, and I knew what would happen next. I was going to have to leave home. Advancement only came from more competition, and I couldn't make that happen living in my small hometown playing against other small towns. I needed to play against the best, and that meant playing with the big boys—the best around in junior hockey. When I look at my daughter today, I can't imagine her leaving home in a couple of years for any reason. But my parents didn't hesitate. I was fifteen years old and asking to leave home, and they said yes.

The year before, I watched one of my friends make it to the Western League as a sixteen-year-old. Moving away from home like that was too much too soon for him, and he wound up coming back. I think he's a teacher now.

I watched him go through all of those ups and downs of making it and then not being able to make it at all, and I got worried. I was going to have to prepare myself if I was going to leave too. The only thing I could think to do was put some walls up around my young teenage heart. My relationship with my parents couldn't stay as close as it had been all my life or it would hurt that much more to leave.

I think they started easing me away, too, because they gave me more and more responsibility that year. Some of it was serious, like when they left me at home for ten days while they went to California, and some of it was more...spontaneous. Like the first time I drove a car. I was fourteen years old. No license, no learning permit. Just me and my dad and the prairies of Alberta late at night.

It happened a couple of games into a junior camp at Medicine Hat, when my dad found out they weren't going to list me.[5] We still had time to fill, and Portland's camp started at eight the next morning. The only thing stopping us from getting there was this crazy seven- or eight-hour drive, overnight, after we had been at the rink all day. Even though he didn't complain, my dad was clearly exhausted. We'd left right from work before driving almost five hundred miles to Medicine Hat and then made it through two days of camp

---

5 There wasn't a draft for juniors, but they could reserve certain players by listing them. The Medicine Hat Tigers didn't think I was a good fit yet, so it was time to hit the road.

before leaving that night for the Portland Winterhawks camp just outside of Edmonton.

About midnight, he looked over at me in the passenger seat and said, "Hey, kid. Can you drive?"

I looked at him, not sure what to say.

"Just keep the car in the middle of the road, and if there are any trucks coming, pull over and go slow."

I thought he would pretend to sleep and still be there to correct my oversteering or give me instructions if something weird came up...but then he started snoring. It was absolutely terrifying. The fear is probably what kept me from falling asleep from boredom on those empty roads. We survived (obviously). I was happy to be able to help my dad after he had done so much for me to get me there, terrified that I would crash and kill us or someone else, and totally exhilarated to actually be driving for real, with no adult supervision.

It wound up being a good thing that we went, too, because that was the camp where Portland listed me. Now there wasn't any doubt I would have to leave home.

For all of the responsibility I felt and the distance I thought I could create, actually leaving wasn't something I could prepare for. Every player who made it would be assigned a billet family who would host them during the season. Standing there at a stranger's house with my hockey bag, crying as my parents drove away, nothing seemed to matter anymore except that I was on my own. What had I gotten myself into?

A few months later, it hadn't gotten better. The tears were still coming as I listened to my parents on the other end of the phone line. I had just finished telling them about how sad I was all the time. How the coach didn't really like me, and I couldn't fit in with the team. How the family I stayed with was nice, but they only had two little babies, and they really had no idea how to feed a growing kid. How I ate a $2.25 poutine special every day for lunch and not much else.[6] How I was out of money and just wanted to come home.

They told me, "Your bedroom is still here. You can come back anytime you want."

I took a big, shaking breath and exhaled my relief. Home was still an option.

Then they had more to say. "But you *do* want to make it to the NHL."

Just like when I was a little kid trying to get on a team, they would never force me to make a decision—but they weren't going to let me forget about my goals either.

"If you come back home to play here, you're not going to get any better. People will remember you quitting that team, and that's not who you are. So you can come home. Just understand what that would mean before you do it."

That's exactly what I needed to hear—that and Mom's promise to send me a couple hundred bucks to get through the rest of the season on a little more than poutine.

It was a tipping point in my life and my career, where I really drew a line in the sand. I hardened my resolve and my commitment. I knew from that moment forward I was all in, with 100 percent dedication, focus, and discipline.

---

6   If you're not Canadian, poutine is a plate of french fries covered in gravy and melted cheese.

I decided right then that I was going to outwork everybody around me. After all, if it were a cakewalk, there's no way I would get stronger. There's no way I could learn the lessons that would carry me through the years of hard coaches and physical disadvantages ahead of me. I had to grow up, and that meant enduring some serious growing pains.

///

That was the year I had my first hockey fight.

In one move, I went from being the best player on the team, the best player in the tournament, and the standout star in the small towns in my area of the country to the youngest guy on a team that didn't even want me there—or at least that's how it felt.

Sure, my work ethic might have been mature enough to leave home, and I was disciplined enough that it was realistic to think I could take my shot to get into the league. But when it came to people, I was still so young and naïve.

My new coach, Wayne Wiemer, never called me any names outright, but he didn't make me feel welcome either. Portland had told him that I was going to play there to develop my skills for next year, and that was that. He was stuck with this too-young, too-scrawny kid who didn't have any of the attributes the other players had. Definitely not the attributes his son Jason had—a highly touted man-child of a sixteen-year-old who was already playing on the Winterhawks. I played on the fourth line with Kimberly unless someone from Portland came to watch. He'd play me more then to make it look like he was developing me, but Wayne Wiemer wanted to win. There were older, stronger, more experienced kids than me, and that's who he was going to play instead of trying to let me grow.

And somehow, I still thought of everyone like I did with my teams back at home: I trusted them all at their word.

It wasn't that I always got along with people. There were plenty of bullies at school growing up. It's just that none of them were on my team. Hockey had been something like a refuge. I could be creative on the ice in a way that I couldn't be anywhere else. Everything went away when I was playing—especially when I got in the zone. So my fights as a kid hadn't come from hockey at all but from a set of brothers back in Hinton.

Looking back, I understand more about how conditions at home can create a bully, and these guys were a perfect example. They didn't have the life or the family that I did. And the one who was in my grade had been held back a couple of years, so all of that hurt and dysfunction was packed into one very large, very angry fourth grader.

Meanwhile, skinny little Dave got ulcers I was so scared of this kid.

It took him picking on a little girl in our grade for me to step up and actually face him. All of the mean things he and his brothers did to me didn't matter, but in my little ten-year-old mind, I was willing to die for this other girl. (Yeah, I had a little bit of a crush too.)

Unfortunately, that happened right in the middle of the school soccer field. Right there in front of everyone, I squared off with the school bully...and I won.

The fight probably looked like this skinny kid was just throwing wild haymaker punches and flailing around while trying not to get killed. But I was just fed up with this guy. Something snapped when he started bothering my friend, and I went after him without any fear.

Humiliating a kid like that is never the end of the story, though, and sure enough, when I got out of school later that day, he was waiting for me with his older *and somehow bigger* brothers. They were lined up in the alleyway that I took to get home, armed with rocks from the gravel road that they fired at me one after the other while I took off running for my life.

Being athletic served me well that day. Rocks whizzed by my head as I ran for my life. As fast as I was, their legs were longer, and I was sure if they caught me, they'd kill me. Down into a local neighborhood, I knew there were certain houses available to us after school, designated as "block parents." These were safe places we could go at any time, and this was *definitely* time. I ran as hard as I could to reach the closest block parent house to us.

Rounding the corner, I finally saw the big red-and-white *Block Parent* sign in the front bay window of a little old lady's house. I slammed into the outside wall, banging on the door and yelling for her to "open up, open up!" Then I dove through to near-safety the second she opened it. I frantically yelled again, "Lock the door! Lock the *door!*" I was still sure they were trying to kill me.

No sooner than she said, "Oh, honey, I'm sure it's not that bad..." rocks started pelting the bay window where the sign was posted.

The police were called. I didn't die, and I thought that was going to be the end of it. But back at school, the principal actually reprimanded *me* for the school field fight—and not the kid who'd been terrorizing the whole school, including the female teachers. When they forced us to shake hands in a fake truce, the kid nearly crushed my hand, and I knew my troubles had only just started.

After that, my dad gave me the green light to fight however I needed to in order to protect myself. Except I still wasn't a fighter—not for myself, anyway. I tried not to cross paths with all the brothers if I could help it, but now I was their focal point. There wasn't a day at that school when I didn't look over my shoulder.

Years later, after I'd been in the NHL for a while, I went back to visit Hinton, my friend Jason, and another friend named Jeff. As one of the only guys who made it out of that rinky-dink town, I felt proud of myself. Like I had become something.

But Jeff didn't show up to the beer gardens when I thought he was going to, and when he did appear, I could tell he was rattled. Something had happened. "You'll never guess," he told me. "I went to grab us a six-pack for later, and when I came out of the liquor store, those guys were there—remember the Beaverbone brothers? Dude, they smashed out my windshield and the lights on my brand-new truck. I'm late because I had to get out of there and call the cops and file a report."

Maybe I didn't feel like fighting them often when I was a kid, but I was ready for it that night. At 220 pounds, I wasn't skinny Dave anymore, and once again they were messing with my friends. We could go and find them. We could make them pay for every second of terror they inflicted when we were kids. Hell, it was almost a decade later, and they were still terrorizing people in that town!

I'd like to say that I've discovered a part of me that wouldn't want to fight them if I ran into them again. I guess it would depend on who needed to be protected. We didn't go out to find a fight that night, but only because Jeff didn't want us to. Injustice—standing up for someone else or sticking up for myself—would make me drop gloves on the ice or go after someone anytime, anyplace. I had a pack mentality that made me loyal to the people around me—nobody messed with my friends, and nobody messed with my teammates. That's what got me into my first of many hockey fights, and that very first one was something to remember.

None of the scuffles that happened in my leagues growing up came with any possibility of getting hurt. When I played, I didn't think about bringing fights into my game at all. But on Wiemer's team, once we made it to juniors, we weren't kids anymore. Along with an increased level of competition came an increased level of aggression too.

One night, the toughest guy in the league started to go after one of our skill guys. All I could see was how little the skill guy was in comparison. Without thinking about it, I yelled at him to "pick on someone his own size." I was tall but rail-thin, and he was 6'5", 225lbs. I didn't really fit the "own size" bill. But all 6'3", 160 pounds of me stepped in to right the injustice anyway.

I didn't even have my gloves off before he pounded me in my face and exploded my nose everywhere. I don't know if I got any punches in at all, but my teammates on the bench were going nuts that I even tried. I had to leave that entire period to clean up all of the blood, but I felt like a good teammate, sticking up for one of my guys, and they were really proud of me for it.

That first broken nose was one of the best things that could have happened to me. My nose was crooked, my face was throbbing, and my coach was smiling. As soon as the game ended, my teammates came running in to hug me and tell me what a great job I did. On the bus home, I basked in the glow of it all. I had fought a giant—and I didn't die. In fact, it made me realize something. If I could fight the toughest guy in the league and take his best punches without it hurting much, I could fight anybody. I felt grateful, confident, and a little bit fearless. Most importantly, I finally felt like I belonged.

I kept it together for the two or three hours back to Kimberly. But when the bus pulled into the parking lot, I hopped into my Dodge Omni to drive back to my billet family's home and let it all out. I shoved a Pearl Jam cassette into the tape deck that was wedged into the console and belted out the song "Alive" at the top of my lungs. I smiled. I cried because of how proud I was of myself and how brave I was becoming. I was grateful, and I felt a shift in my perspective on life. Nothing was holding me back anymore.

Fighting was never pleasant—at least it never was for me— but at least I wasn't afraid of it anymore. Some guys grow to love that part of the game. That's not my story. On nights when I knew I was going to have to fight, I'd think about it all day long, with butterflies in my stomach, anxiousness, and sometimes anxiety trying to take over my mind and body. There's always potential to get seriously hurt or embarrassed in front of a crowd and a TV audience. Imagine standing up in the middle of your workday to see a stadium of 18,000 people all cheering you on and screaming their faces off during a fight.

Now imagine your job is to fight other well-conditioned enforcers and gladiators, with all of those people watching you put your life and reputation on the line.

It's kind of crazy now that I think about it. There's always a potential that you'll seriously hurt yourself or someone else. After that first fight broke the proverbial ice (by breaking my actual face), it became doable, but never enjoyable.

Although...damn. Nothing else could get the crowd to their feet like a good fight.

///

After that bloody nose, I changed a little bit in Coach Wiemer's eyes. Honestly, I changed in my own eyes too. My chest stuck out a little bit further, and I stood up a little bit straighter. It left me with a don't-fuck-with-me attitude that wound up serving me well. When I dropped gloves and one-punched a kid who had a reputation for fighting dirty, I started to get more ice time. Wiemer wanted to see me get more aggressive, and that's what I was doing. If I could play the role that he was looking for, even if it wasn't in my nature, he would give me more ice time.

That's probably when it dawned on me that we were playing for jobs. It wasn't kid stuff anymore. Being aggressive, playing like the coach wanted me to play, outworking anyone around me—that's the kind of thing that was going to build a career. I didn't have a choice about how I played or whether I got in fights. Not if I wanted to make it. Not if I wanted to get to the next level. If I wasn't scoring or setting up goals for my teammates, then I needed to be a wrecking ball out there, hitting and fighting anything that moved. I needed people to notice me every game, some way or somehow. So that's what I did. Game after game.

If I hadn't learned how to hit or to stay high energy or play a physical game, I never would have made it out of juniors.

That lesson is ultimately what earned me a spot on the Winterhawks—that and the twenty-three goals I was able to score for Kimberly once I settled in. Then they let me come down to Portland from Kimberly, presumably to play for the Winterhawks. But when I got down there, three or four other guys were also waiting—too many to play in one game. I watched them play the Seattle Thunderbirds from the stands, with a jersey that had a misspelled name, before riding back to Portland with the team I wasn't sure I was on.[7]

During morning skate the next day, I hustled. I wanted to play that night, and I knew that meant I needed to show them I was all in. But when they called everyone off the ice except for six names, and mine was one of them, my heart sank. We had just done forty-five minutes of tough conditioning, and the other guys were all taking off for lunch and an afternoon nap before the game. Keeping us out there with the assistant coach—no head coach or GM standing by—couldn't be good.

Without an explanation, he started skating us in sprints back and forth across the ice. Over and over again, we kept skating, harder and harder, knowing it was a game day, feeling

---

7   The jersey they handed me misspelled my name as Scratchhand, which the team and some of the other guys teased me about. I decided to have them remove the name tag rather than have the wrong name, but that didn't go over well either. In hindsight, it would have been better to play as a healthy Scratchhand than to be the rookie with a blank jersey!

every second of our hour and a half and counting on the ice, without an end in sight.

The coach was yelling at us, telling us to push ourselves, but we were exhausted after the morning skate we'd just finished. Some of the guys started whispering that we should just pace ourselves. If we all slowed it down, we might make it. We needed a break.

A huge, reasonable part of me wanted to save my energy for the next time I actually got to practice or play. But this strong inner voice told me to bury the guys next to me. I listened. Nobody was in shape like I was, and I didn't want to back off. Everyone else could try to keep up with me if they wanted to, but I knew one thing for sure: I was going to skate my heart out.

Boards to boards, line to line, lap by lap, I made a conscious decision to finish each lap at full speed, all out.

Blue line to red line. Red line to blue line. Far end, back. Blue line, back. Goal line, back. I skated until my legs burned and my stomach threatened to toss everything from that morning's breakfast back up onto the ice. A few guys did rush over to the bench to puke their brains out, but I kept pushing. Back and forth we kept going, and I kept outworking, out-hustling everyone around me.

I pushed the pace. The coach kept it going. I showed off the conditioning I'd gained from the extra training I did with all my lonely free time. I showed them I'd outwork anyone to earn and keep my spot. The whistle kept blowing. The skate kept going. By the end, I was lapping guys. By the end, every single ounce of me had been poured out onto the ice.

The whistle came in a few short bursts, and it was finally over. I couldn't have skated harder. I couldn't have shown that

I wanted it more. All of our lungs burned, and our legs were seizing up. But it was my shoulders that the coach wrapped his arm around. Out of all the guys skating, I was the only one who heard the words: "You're playing tonight." A couple of them were sent back to sit out the upcoming game. Three of them were sent back home to Canada.

The whole thing had been a test. The GM and head coach weren't there because they had been watching from the rafters. How we responded to this challenge helped them make their final decision.

I was two people away from going home that night, and who knows what would have transpired after that. If I hadn't skated as hard as I possibly could, my whole life might have been different. Instead, I was going to play—just hours after I skated harder than I ever had in my life. The coach knew that, and I played on the fourth line without a huge amount of playing time. But my work had already been done. I showed them what I could do. I set the tone for the rest of my career. I would be a relentless worker, always pushing to work harder and get better. I wouldn't be the most gifted goal scorer or stick handler, but few people would ever outwork me.

Pieces of that lesson still hold true today: you can't confuse the dream with the shiny fun benefits of the dream. Sometimes it hurts. A lot. But when you think you can't go any further, there's almost always something else inside of you that can push just a little bit more.

I knew then what my parents knew about me back when I called them hoping to come home: it didn't matter what path I had to take to get into the NHL, as long as I actually made it.

I'm grateful to my dad for teaching me how to identify what I needed to do to improve. I'm grateful for my time with Wayne Wiemer and the coaches who pushed me to my max and beyond. They made my life hell for a while, but if I hadn't learned to adapt then, there's no way I would have made it later on in the NHL. I wouldn't have made it there at all.

CHAPTER THREE

I'LL PLAY TILL I DIE

×

If Kimberly had been difficult to adapt to, Portland seemed impossible. This kid from a town of six thousand people, transplanted into a city of millions, felt more out of place than ever. My billet family lived forty-five minutes from the practice rink, and every day I'd drive my used '84 Trans Am down the wrong exit on their complicated freeway system.[8] To top it all off, our red Winterhawks gear put us right in the middle of the Bloods and Crips feuds that raged throughout the nineties. It was a completely different world.

---

8   Just picture it: copper-beige with flip-up lights, just like Knight Rider.

I had skipped two grades by getting ahead earlier in high school, so while I was in town anyway, I enrolled at Portland State University. The team was great about keeping kids' school going while they were playing, so practices began around one every afternoon in order to accommodate morning classes. We would do our homework on the bus during our long Western Hockey League road trips while traveling to one of seventy-two games a year, with some trips as long as twenty-four hours on the bus.

Halfway through that first year, we had to make one of those twenty-four-hour bus rides to Manitoba for our eastern swing road trip. Squashed up against the window with a much bigger player on the other side of me the whole ride, sleep wasn't happening for me. After what seemed like the longest night ever, we finally made it there, played our games, and then started the long drive back. By then, I was dead tired, and my throat had started to hurt too.

As I struggled to get comfortable enough to sleep, the GM called me up to the front of the bus and asked what was going on. "Based on the way you've played, there'd better be something wrong with you," he warned, "or you're going home."

The verdict for my throat was a severe strep infection. But there was more, too. My spleen had enlarged to three or four times its normal size, and I had a confirmed case of mononucleosis. If I played again too soon, my spleen could actually rupture. So you could say the upside was that I *definitely* had something wrong with me. I wasn't going home, but I wasn't doing much else, either.

For twenty-some hours of the day, I'd sleep like a rock. In the little bit of time I was awake, I'd swig cough syrup just to coat my throat enough to get some water down. My roommate, tough guy Dave Cammock, brought me cough drops, but I didn't eat much else. I did this for three weeks, barely eating and trying not to dehydrate in the few hours I could stay awake. Without the calories and workouts, I lost weight that I didn't have to lose. Down to 155, 150, 145...

I was gaunt, gross, and miserable. And I still wanted to play.

As soon as I could get a little food in me, my coach, Brent Peterson, gave me a training plan that started completely from scratch. It started with just five minutes on the Stairmaster, which was all I could manage. Slowly, I built up to ten, then fifteen, then thirty minutes at a time.

After two or three months off the ice and weeks spent half dead in my room, I finally managed to get back to myself just before the end of the season. In fact, I was able to work out in the gym weeks before I could get back on the ice, and I actually got really strong.

I wasn't playing as much as I would have liked, but I was playing my ass off. Toward the end of the season, there was an injury to one of the top lines. I was bumped up to play with future NHLer and first-round draft pick Adam Deadmarsh and a talented sniper named Lonny Bohonos. They would be the skill, but my physical play and tenacity opened up the ice for them. We finished strong, and I had a great playoffs that salvaged my season and my draft year.

That's when the scouts found me again—but they were different this time. Near the end of the season, my very first scout took me and my parents out to dinner at the Red Lion Hotel in Portland. I think his name was Garth Malarchuk, and he asked me if I had any representation yet. I didn't.

"It's time to get him an agent," he told my parents. "He's going to be drafted."

After all of the sickness and injury and falling so far behind, somehow I actually had a shot. Not a great one—I was ranked at 168, which still means a fifth- or sixth-round pick and no guarantee of actually playing up in the league. But I was definitely getting noticed.

After that, I decided to keep doing the things that seemed to be working. I didn't take any time off. I stayed in the gym and kept building muscle. When Central Scouting fitness tests came around a month or two after the season, I drove down to Vancouver with a bunch of guys who were expected to be high draft picks. Guys I'd played against and knew were going to be great. But because of how hard I had been training, I knew they were nowhere as fit as me.

I crushed it. My VO2 run on the bike even gathered a little crowd of scouts watching as I clocked a sixty-nine (anything over sixty was considered exceptional, especially on the bike). By the end, my physical fitness test results were number one in the world, and my overall ranking pulled up from the projection of 168 in the world at Christmas to 68 after playoffs and Central Scouting. Not only was I going to be drafted, but I needed to get my first nice suit. I was going to go much earlier than I thought.

Before the draft, I met with seven or eight NHL teams. They stripped me down to my underwear and searched my body for scars and injuries. They shook down my character, making accusations to see how I'd react. They started telling me that they had heard I liked to drink, which was the furthest thing from the truth. I laughed and told them they had the wrong guy—I had probably only had a couple of beers in my lifetime up to that point. They were just probing, something they would do with every guy to see how we would react or to find out if there was any truth to their accusations. Then they ran psychological tests and physical tests and asked so many questions.

But there was one question I knew how to answer as soon as it was asked: "What happens if you start in the minors?"

I didn't hesitate. "Then I'll play in the minors."

It came from the assistant GM of the Vancouver Canucks—George McPhee, now the GM for the Las Vegas Golden Knights—and he pushed me a little further. He said, "But how long would you want to play there?"

"As long as it takes. I'll play till I die."[9]

He thought for a moment and then said, "Listen. I've interviewed twenty guys today. That's the best answer we've had so far."

The next day, Brad Symes, a friend and teammate in Portland, and I went down to Hartford, Connecticut, together for the draft. He was supposed to be the big star going in the first round, and I was excited to just be moving up from the bottom. Player after player went as we listened for his name... but then mine came first. Forty-second overall as the Canucks' second pick. That same year, Mattias Öhlund was selected in the first round. We wound up becoming lifelong friends.

---

9   I'm not sure I knew how serious that statement was. In 2011, the year I ultimately retired due to concussion issues, three players in four months died by suicide with CTE. Brad Symes, who shows up in the next couple of paragraphs, was always a fighter when we were playing. He died by suicide as well.

Nothing about that moment felt real. I remember it through a fog. I was called up on stage, with the Hartford Civic Center filled with fans and players. Someone handed me a jersey, and everyone took pictures. Someone else guided me to a media person taking even more pictures. Then there was Pat Quinn, the GM for the Canucks, all of the press, and so many amazing people surrounding us. I signed a deal for hockey cards right then, with someone who sent 7,500 hockey cards for me to sign. Later that year, they wound up spread out in stacks and boxes all over my parents' house during the Christmas holiday—evidence that all the sacrifices had been worth it.

///

The draft was a shock that turned 1994 into a blur. Even though I would still play on the Winterhawks for another year, it felt different. I felt different. I had been *drafted*. A year before, I had been struggling just to make the team. Now, I was the captain.

When I was a kid, I would analyze the drafted players. I would track their stats so closely and watch every move they made on the ice. I wanted to know what it looked like to be a first-rounder or a third-rounder. I wanted to know so that I could do it too.

Now that it was me out there, I was the one to analyze. It began to turn into a head game more than a celebration. I started to believe everyone was judging me as a high second-round pick. Instead of emulating me, I believed they were critical of me. Every move I made, every play I was part of, I put under a microscope. I could hear people in the stands, on my team, even in my family being disappointed in me.

I heard the Canucks telling me that I was going to be a project but that they liked my potential—and then completely revised that in my mind so that I believed there were high expectations I would have to live up to. Like everyone was shaking their heads, saying, "I can't believe that guy went forty-second in the world."

I worried that I got picked higher than I should have been, and I worried that I might let down the people who believed in me.

The games kept coming through another year with the Winterhawks, and I was even made team captain. At the end of our season in juniors, Syracuse called me up. They were the Canucks' farm team, and they wanted me to go there to skate with the team and be available in case there were any injuries during their playoff run.

No one was judging me. No one was disappointed in me. I was eighteen and on the ice for playoff games in the pros. No unreasonable expectations, no worries, no distractions. It was just me and hockey.

///

For the first few months, I slept in a hotel, but I lived at the rink. I was there to learn what it was like to be a pro and to keep improving, training, and getting better. But I was naïve, and there were other things going on that I was oblivious to. Guys with families and contracts were furious because our Canadian Canucks contracts translated to about half their worth in New York. Because our team was playing well and making a deep playoff run, guys were extending their leases, paying more rent, and paying hotel bills while realizing the owner would not be giving out typical playoff bonus checks to cover their expenses. Instead, he chose to give the guys watches. *Watches.* Needless to say, watches don't pay the bills—and neither do postseason games.

The closer we got to the end of the year, the more furious some of the older players became. Without me even being aware of it, a few players on the team—mostly older career minor leaguers—thought that they would be better off if we lost out sooner rather than later to avoid having to pay for another month's rent or hotel rooms and bills. Just quit trying. End the run.

I can honestly say it was the first and only time I saw players at any level quit playing hard. No one gets paid a salary once the season ends, and they weren't getting bonuses to make up for it. If management didn't care to pay them, then management didn't need wins in return.

Naïve as I was, I missed all of this. Coming from the juniors, where we only got paid gas money, I was happy just to be there. Bonus money meant nothing to me. So I played my heart out as usual, even though the long-time pros were trying to make a statement.

But I had made the decision to keep outworking everyone else. It didn't matter what they were doing; it wasn't going to change me or how I played. It wasn't going to affect my field or distract me from my mission. I was trying to make it to the NHL as quickly as possible.

I took that same energy into the Canucks' camp later that year. I was in training camp with Tyson Nash, Brian Loney, and a guy a couple of years older than us who had played up a little the year before and was sure he was destined to make it.

Before training camp, I had fallen over a goalie while demonstrating a drill teaching hockey school and subluxated my shoulder. My game had to change a little, especially if I was going to keep it quiet. I focused on a skills game instead of the tough-guy fighting routine I'd been doing.[10]

Nash and I felt great about the whole camp. In the cab on the way back to the airport, Nash and I were pumped up, sure that our stay in Syracuse would be worth it—that we would be the first guys called up if there were injuries on the Canucks.

Then Loney turned around from the front seat of the cab and hit us with a jaded reality check: "You guys are fourth-liners who don't score. They only kept you around because you work so fucking hard. They don't actually want you. There's no way either of you actually makes the NHL."

I didn't know whether to cry or punch him in the face.

So instead, I used his words as fuel and motivation. I made it my mission to get called up before Loney.[11]

///

Back in Syracuse, Nash and I got an apartment together to save a few hundred bucks a month. We saved even more by getting a crappy little apartment on the top floor of a crappy little building. Then we pieced together furniture like you'd expect

---

10 When I couldn't bench press in the fitness test, the trainers found out about my shoulder and were furious. I wasn't really trying to hide it from them—I just thought it would get better and be fine.

11 In the end, Brian Loney wound up playing a total of twelve games in the NHL. He was never called up again after that training camp and the comments that he made. Funny how karma works—Tyson Nash and I finished with over a thousand combined games.

a couple of broke kids to do—we had no bed frames, and our mattresses were awful. Our dining room table was a Ping-Pong table. Our oven wasn't reliable, and the heater didn't work at all, so we left the oven door open to heat the house. We had a coffee table made from broken hockey sticks, and we had a pet squirrel in the attic.

Tyson was the king of beating the system and getting a deal, so he thought it would be a good idea to buy a TV-VCR combo at the WIZ, which had a sixty-day return policy. He wanted to buy one and return it for a full refund on day sixty, and then I would buy another for the next sixty days and return mine. That way, we could get through the whole year without actually buying a TV.

We also found out that the best spot for dinner was Olive Garden because of the extra salad and breadsticks. We'd alternate whose "birthday" it was now and then to get some dessert too. And we saved about fifty bucks a month by moving heavy stuff like freezers and stoves for the other tenants moving in and out of the building. We paid for it in back pain, at least for the first few practices.

It was the best time.

And it wasn't going to last. That season in Syracuse got cut short, not because I got called up. Not because I wasn't playing well, but because something was wrong with my feet.

My feet felt like they were going to shatter, and come to find out, that's actually what the doctors told me could happen. For whatever reason, my heels were hollow, like blown-out eggshells. The doctors weren't sure if it was a genetic defect or because of injuring my heels when I was younger. Regardless, they told me it was a one-in-a-million condition, and if I wanted to keep playing, they'd have to scrape some bone out of my hip and then graft it into my heels.

Recovery in Vancouver, where they flew me back for surgery, was harder than I could have imagined. I woke up to all these staples on my hip and bandages around my feet. And then the worst part of it all started almost immediately—this terrible cramp that ran from my lower quad up into my psoas muscle and my lower abs. I remember sweating profusely, stuck with my leg extended and flexed so hard that I felt it all in my stomach, hip, and leg. Because I was dehydrated from the anesthesia, it nearly became a total body cramp. It was the worst pain I have ever felt.

My dad was a pretty hard-ass guy, but even he struggled to see me in that kind of agony. No matter what kind of medicine they gave me, no matter how we massaged it, the cramp and the pain would not subside. After a half hour without any kind of relief, I almost passed out from exhaustion. Just being stuck in that position, outside of my will, for that long was work. The pain made it that much worse.

That terrible post-op moment set me up for some of the scariest moments of my early career. I wasn't even sure I was going to have a career after that. It took two more surgeries on my heels for the doctors to feel that it would be safe for me to try to play again. I'd crawl from the bed to the bathroom in my hotel—the Rosedale on Robson Suites—as few times a day as I could. I'd give the bellman my room key so he could bring room service to my bed. A wheelchair wasn't even an option because the doctors and trainers were concerned about my legs atrophying.

There was nothing I could do but lie in bed and make deals with God to protect my future in hockey.

If you get me out of this thing, I'll work my ass off.

I'll never be lazy again.

I'll be a good guy all the time, I swear!

As soon as I could hobble around on crutches in the gym, I started working out my upper body. The surgeries had happened at the end of one Canucks season, but now the next was looming. With training camp approaching fast, there wasn't much time left to try to make the team, and my legs were getting smaller and smaller. That made the news from the doctor so much worse. Instead of being cleared to skate, there had been a mistake. We had to do yet another surgery, six weeks before camp.

With barely enough time to get on my feet at all, I pushed through the pain and did what I could to make it to camp. My whole life had led to this moment, this season where I could finally realize my childhood dream and make it to the NHL, and I hadn't even been on the ice since Christmas. But I couldn't do it alone—quite literally. My skates didn't fit right. They had packed the cavity of my heels full of ground-up donor bone, and it pushed everything out in odd places. The new, temporarily misshapen bone structure pressed through the skin, through the stitches, and made the heels of my feet too bulky for the skates.

I finally got the Canuck trainers Pat O'Niell and Darren Granger to modify a pair of skates for me. They heated the heels up so that we could punch out that part of the skate boot where the extra bone had been packed in all lumpy and weird.

It was enough to get me back on the ice, though it would still be painful for months. Among other injuries, those small but significant traumas before and during my career wouldn't fully release until the healing work I did long after it all ended.

I didn't think I had any chance of making the team that year, and I still don't know how it really happened. But somehow, after sticking to my motto of doing something to get noticed every game—hitting, fighting, scoring—I found myself on the team's roster at the end of training camp. We were heading to Japan to start the 1997–98 hockey season. With my car still parked on the curb in Syracuse, I went straight from surgery to camp and now to Japan for the Canucks' first games. And I never looked back.

CHAPTER FOUR

THE KID'S DREAMS COME TRUE

X

I wasn't sure at first if they were going to keep me. Being on the bubble was Portland all over again, and I felt like I was on the outside looking in. The first games that the Canucks played that year were in Japan, and they were the first NHL games to ever be played outside of North America. It was us against the Anaheim Ducks, with a sixteen-hour time change to adapt to. And I was only there because they were allowed to carry a couple of extra players with them in case someone got hurt.

The plane to Japan was the biggest one I'd ever been on. Our seats were upstairs, and I'd never even seen a plane with two levels.

All of the veterans on the team were taking sleeping stuff and getting ready to sleep on the flight so they'd be awake when we got there. I, on the other hand, thought taking something might throw off my game, even though we weren't playing for four or five days, and they knew how to handle this sort of thing better than me. I was trying to be smart. I could make it work without messing with my system.

So I didn't sleep almost the whole flight. On purpose.

When we landed, it felt like we took a huge jump into the future. A day and night had gone missing, and we had to adjust enough to play well in just a few days. Our doctors and trainers suggested staying out as late as we could to help us adjust to the time, and the best way to do that was to hit Roppongi in downtown Tokyo.

Roppongi feels a lot like Times Square, with the lights and nightlife and so many people. But the technology was ten years ahead of anything we had in Canada or the states. Where we were just coming out with Motorola flip phones, they had tiny little phones that hung from necklaces. The food was amazing. The energy was incredible. And our designated tour guide who stayed with us kept up drinking with two-hundred-plus-pound guys until his immaculate suit turned into a tie wrapped around his head like Mr. Miyagi.

Jet-lagged and exhausted, we collapsed into bed after the first night out and then had a light practice the next day. Each day got a little more intense as we built our energy back up for the game.

We were playing in the Yoyogi Arena, which had been built for the Olympics that Japan had hosted back in the sixties. It was huge, but it was a multipurpose arena that was primarily used for swimming. The rink was built up over the top of the pool, with high-dive boards just behind the nets. The whole thing was surreal. They had done so much to accommodate us as the first NHL game outside of North America that they rolled out the red carpet for us every event leading up to the night of the games.

Mark Messier was a celebrity, of course, as a Hall of Famer, and Paul Kariya was supposed to come as the draw from the Mighty Ducks but didn't make it because of a contract dispute. But they embraced all of us, excited to show us everything about their culture and to get just a piece of us as well.

The second night there, we were taken to a big reception dinner, with all of these important people in attendance. There were women dressed in gorgeous kimonos. The music was beautiful, and the spread of sushi was unbelievable. The third night, I was rooming with Mess, and he brought me along to a dinner with about five other players, someone with lots of secret service who honestly might have been the prime minister of Japan...and me. They closed down the whole restaurant for us, which was already hidden and clearly high-end.

I knew it was going to be crazy when the guy at the teppan-yaki grill reached into a bucket and threw out a handful of live prawns, which began running around all over the hot grill.

The government official laughed while the chef chopped the prawns into pieces on the grill and piled up the heads on one side with their tentacles still moving and eyeballs bulging out of their skulls. "You like dessert?" he asked. "Best part. Like popcorn!"

The guys all turned to me. "You're first, Scatch!"

I swallowed and tried not to grimace—I couldn't be the rookie who let them down.

And if I didn't think about eating tiny little brains, I had to say: it did taste like popcorn.

///

After practice the next day, one of the PR guys for the event asked me if I could help them out with something. The National Japanese Roller Hockey team had put up a rink outside of the Yoyogi Stadium, and they wanted guys to make an appearance, sign some autographs, and pass the puck around with the roller hockey team. One of the guys who was supposed to be there couldn't make it, so they wanted me to fill his spot. I was up for anything, so I put on my suit, threw a jersey over it, and joined the guys following NHL security through the crowd.

No one noticed us at first—the people who were there were all watching the guys in full gear whipping around inside the in-line skating rink. So we crossed the barrier and joined them, running around in our dress shoes, ripping shots on the goalies, and passing the pucks to the guys on the team.

A crowd started to form, and forty-five minutes later we were taking pictures, signing things, and having a blast making a buzz for their team and our upcoming game. We didn't realize just how big the crowd had gotten until it was time to get off the rink and get back to the complex.

It was too tight to move.

Security took the most famous players out first, escorting them across the four-hundred-yard walk back to the complex. People were reaching around security, grabbing and pulling and trying to touch the guys. Each time they came back for another group, the crowd became more fearless, holding out Sharpies for autographs and hitting us with them instead, reaching for our faces, yelling and screaming like we were the Beatles.

I stood back and watched in awe. A couple of years before, I'd been playing junior hockey, and now I was about to sprint through a crowd of Japanese people who just wanted to say they got a hand on me. I was even more shocked when the PR team handed me an envelope filled with cash—about $5,000—thanked me, and left.

Welcome to the NHL, kid. What a way to set the tone for my career.

For all of the fun, food, and opportunities, it still didn't feel real until I walked into the dressing room and saw a Canucks jersey waiting with my name on it. That wasn't just a jersey. It was everything I had busted my ass for my whole life. Every rainy day, every snowstorm, every run through the woods in the summer. Every teacher who told me to have a backup plan because I couldn't actually go pro. Every time Loney's words echoed around in my brain, telling me I wasn't good enough and would never make it. All of it was wrapped up in that one jersey and the unexpected opportunity to play that night.

Mike Sillinger had come expecting to play, but at the end of practice, our goalie, Artūrs Irbe, accidentally collided with him while they were practicing shootout moves. Silly needed twenty-five stitches to stop the bleeding. His injury turned into my opportunity.

For years, I had promised my parents that I would bring them to my first game in the NHL. Since I couldn't bring them with me to Japan, I'd bought them a giant TV before I left. I think they still have it. As the Canadian and American anthems played and the Japanese fans cheered for everyone on both teams, I was so glad I had. I knew my parents were watching when my name was called and I lined up to play.

It felt like electricity shooting through my body, building up to send me flying across the ice.

I jumped over the boards.

My skates hit the ice.

I had made it.

///

Playing actually felt easier in the NHL. Everyone knew the right play to make at the right time. I wasn't constantly trying to cover for people who weren't as skilled or were still working on their craft. There was a certain comfort in knowing I just had to do my job and everyone else would do theirs too.

For a while, everything was fresh and exciting. There was my first time playing in front of my family. The first time playing a home game and showing Vancouver fans what I could do. My first fight in the NHL, first goal in the NHL, first road trip, and everything I'd dreamed about doing my whole life. Every stadium was different. Some of them, like the LA Forum and New York's iconic Madison Square Garden, were especially cool because you would look into the stands and see your favorite

celebrities cheering you on. Some of them were historic, changing in dressing rooms that every player who had ever played the
game had changed in. Skating on ice where blood and guts and
sweat and work had been poured out for fifty years. Every city
was a new adventure, better than anything I thought it could be.

I wasn't playing for the money. I was playing to feed my soul.

But while $5,000 for playing with some kids outside of an
arena was fun, money was still a reality. During my first years
in the NHL, I was one of the lowest-paid guys in the league,
and I didn't know how long it would last. I tried to save as
much money as possible, and Peter Shaefer, a knockout star
in juniors, had an uncle with a basement suite open near the
practice arena. He let me rent it out for a few hundred bucks a
month—just a bed, a mini kitchen at the end of the room, and
a tiny bathroom that put your feet almost in the shower basin
when you sat on the toilet.

For the next month and half, I stayed in that tiny basement
apartment and drove in every night to hang out with first-round-
pick Mattias and the other young guys in downtown Vancouver.
After dinner and staying out, I'd crash with him in the townhouse he was renting downtown on the seawall by the marina.
Eventually, he asked me if I wanted to room with him—no
charge. My salary was almost the same as one of his paychecks,
but I kept offering to pay him anyway. He kept refusing to take
it. I think I bought him a VCR that year as a rent payment.

While I didn't have much salary to work with compared to a
lot of the guys in the league, none of it mattered to me. At twen-
ty-one, I was making more money than I had ever imagined to
play a game that I would have played for free.

Back in juniors, when I got my signing bonus after the draft, there was only one thing I really wanted to do with that money: buy my first nice car.

I drove my old '84 Trans Am up to Vancouver, and my parents drove down from Salmon Arm to meet me. Together, we found the perfect car, owned by the lot that my friend's dad worked for. It wasn't new, and it wasn't the most expensive ever, but it was going to be mine. A twin-turbo, six-speed, Dodge Stealth.[12] Never mind the fact that I couldn't drive a stick and I'd just had thumb surgery. It was going to take something bigger than a thumb to keep me down. I would try to get onto Team Canada for the World Junior Championships with that same cast on a couple of months later. I didn't make the team, but I could figure out how to drive a car.

The dealer must have cringed as I hopped into the Stealth to drive it away—left-handed, with my casted nub on the steering wheel and my other hand crossed over to shift. It was a gorgeous car that called everyone's attention to it...and there I went, lurching and stalling all over the road. I laughed as much as I bet the guys on the lot were laughing at me too.

The weirder part for me was being able to buy the thing in the first place. I was used to limits and just getting by, not walking into a dealership and walking out with the exact car I wanted. Growing up, if I wanted new hockey equipment, I had to work up the money to buy it. Sure, my parents would chip in here and there if things got really tough, but for the most part, I learned to be self-reliant. For a kid with ambitions, that means

---

12 This was before the Viper came out.

learning how to either get by with what you have or wheel and deal to get to the next level.

The earliest hustle I remember working up was back when everyone played marbles in elementary school. I always had my eye out for that one marble that could take down the rest and add to my collection. And I found this certain kind of Christmas decoration that was perfect. They were see-through, hard, acrylic balls that people would just set out in baskets or on mantles or something silly. Like most kids my age, I didn't really care about home décor. All I saw was the perfect shooter: small enough to shoot but big enough that it would hit all of the other marbles, which of course means you get to win them. I called them Super Jumbos.

With a couple of new Super Jumbos in hand, I set out to play and, just like I imagined, started winning all these marbles. That got the other kids' attention, who all wanted to know where they could get Super Jumbos too.

"Sure, I could get a couple for you!" I'd promise. "They're two dollars each, but that's nothing for all the marbles you can win with a Super Jumbo."

The next day at school, they'd show up with a couple bucks in hand and dreams of winning big in mind.

My buddy and I had a whole box of them to sell, but I knew that if we let them all go at once, they wouldn't mean as much anymore. So I rationed them out slowly. "I found one more, guys! Five bucks for the last one." Then a little while later I'd *discover* another small stash and drip them into our little market. I'm not sure what ten-year-old thinks like that, but it felt like a game that was almost better than marbles.

As I got bigger, so did the ways I could make money. I ran a paper route on my roller blades from the ages of ten to twelve, rode my bike to work at McDonald's for a couple of years after I turned fourteen, and worked harder than anyone else at Safeway from seventeen to nineteen. I was the kid everyone knew would run through the aisles to get a price check and bag groceries with a smile, and it was exactly the kind of work ethic they wanted to see. That last summer, after the draft but before I'd made it onto the Canucks, the city of Salmon Arm hired me.

As the youngest guy on staff with the city, I got a lot of the crappy jobs that the other guys didn't want. For example, every morning at four thirty, I'd drive a truck that had an extension wand mounted to the side of it to water the baskets of flower arrangements hanging from the streetlamps around town. Later, I'd clean up the parks and beaches, pick up trash, mow sports fields, and clean out bathrooms. I had all that time to myself, feeling some pride in what I was doing, and then my afternoons were totally free so I could train and work out for two to three hours. It was perfect.

I remember one morning, about a month into the job, I was driving back to the main service garage when the cab of my truck lit up with smoke...and foam. I reflexively hit the windshield wipers, but of course nothing happened since it was all on the inside of the vehicle. So I frantically wiped down the glass in front of me with my hands, just to see enough that I didn't crash. Fortunately, I was close enough to the garage that I didn't have far to go. Unfortunately, I was close enough to the main service garage that everyone there saw the whole thing.

Apparently, when I slid my left foot back from the pedals to rest it near the seat, I must have hit the fire extinguisher at the same time. When I pulled up to the maintenance garage, I fell out of the truck, covered in white stuff, to see the guys rolling on the ground with tears in their eyes they were laughing so hard.

"Maybe you should stick to hockey, kid. Leave the hard stuff to us!"

"Yeah, like driving!"

///

That Stealth, once I learned to drive it, became the center of so many memories. Some silly, some crazy...and some deeply painful.

Trevor Linden, the Canucks team captain, had close ties to the Ronald McDonald house in Vancouver, where families would stay while kids went through treatment for cancer and other terrible illnesses. Not long into my time in Vancouver, I got connected with the work he was doing and fell in love right away. I wasn't a whole lot older than some of the kids there, but I felt drawn to them. I couldn't fix what was wrong, but I could help them out while they were there.

You could feel the pressure of worry and anxiety in the parents and kids in the house. All of these little angels were fighting terrible diseases, and their parents were quitting jobs and doing what they could to take care of them. One little boy stood out in particular, and we came to be good friends. He was like a little brother. His name was Nicholas.

Nicholas was twelve, and he loved cars like I did. He loved big machinery, too, and anything else that had a motor in it. After a few months of hanging out around the Ronald McDonald House, I asked his mom if I could take him for a ride in my Stealth—that dream car that I had been so excited to buy. She said okay, and we went down to an abandoned parking lot by the ocean. After having a blast on our joyride down there, I asked him if he was ready.

Then I raised the seat up, switched spots, and belted him in. "Let's go!"

For the next thirty minutes, he ripped around the parking lot, totally loving the power of the turbos and just how fast he could go in it. We raced around, screaming and laughing and going *so* fast. Honestly, he was way better with the manual transmission than I was my first time out. So I turned to him again and told him, "That was a pretty good test, man."

"What do you mean?"

"I mean now we can take this on the road. Go ahead. You're doing great."

There aren't a lot of open highways in Vancouver, but we pulled onto a quieter stretch of road, and again he did great. We kept going into the city, a young kid and his car, with an even younger kid in the driver's seat, having the time of our lives.

I can't honestly tell you how long Nicholas and I hung out together—a couple of years at least. We went driving more, in parking lots and shipyards, having conversations about life and girls and things he might talk to a big brother about. When he passed away, it broke my heart so much that I blocked out a lot of it just to keep from hurting.

A few years later, I connected with another amazing little man—Adam Novellano—this time in Long Island after I got traded to the Islanders. He loved playing video games. His brothers and I would play street hockey while he cheered us on, and then he and I would go inside and play his hockey video game.

"The kid shoots and scores!" One of us was always yelling about it, whether it was me about my real self or him about my EA Sports character. When they started making NHL games, I got to help them design some of the specs, how players moved and skated, and where they passed the puck. To this day, people will tell me how my character was their secret weapon on their favorite version of those games. I tend to believe that the developers made me and the other guys who chipped in a little more powerful in exchange for the help. So when Adam and I played NHL at his house, he would sometimes choose me as a player to play against me in real life.

Those visits were full of so much life and joy and fun that it was hard to remember why I was there in the first place. After a practice one night, someone caught me and delivered the devastating news: my little buddy was gone.

As soon as I could, I got back out to his place to support the remaining Novellano brothers. We even played a street hockey game in his memory.[13] I didn't have anyone to play with when we lost Nicholas, but I dedicated a game to him and scored two goals against the Boston Bruins in his honor. These aren't huge

---

13 My heart still breaks when I think about Adam and the life he could have led. One of his brothers wrote about that day in a piece that's archived here: *https://www.dbstalk.com/community/index.php?threads/ dave-scatchard-my-brother-and-the-kid-new-york-islanders- feature.9132/*

gestures in the scheme of things, but what can any of us do in the face of that kind of heartbreak?

I know what I did. The same thing I did for all the dislocations and breaks and concussions and physical pain I felt year after year: shove it down and don't think about it.

Don't think about how skinny they look after chemo and how it looks like the doctors are killing them instead of saving them. Don't think about how terrible people get more time on this planet than these little angels or how much pain they had to experience in what little time they did get.

I never really went back to hanging out with sick kids after that. I wasn't sure how to cope with that kind of grief without getting lost in it. It felt like too much to even take a moment to appreciate how cool it was that we got some time with these kids at all. That they could share their light and joy with us before going back to the other side and that we could love them and learn from them in the meantime.

Those two little dudes carried me over a bridge between rookie and hometown bliss to the colder realizations of life in the league. They stayed with me forever—buried deep inside for a long, long time. It's still hard to think about the lives they should have gotten, but I'm grateful to have shared some small part with them and their amazing families anyway.

///

After so many years of sacrifice and support, I loved sharing my success with my parents. When I took my parents out to amazing, fancy dinners after I made it to the NHL, I thought about my mom sending me cash for food back when I was sixteen. I thought about those Christmas gifts that anchored my love for hockey every time I could spend money on them. And more than anything, I wanted to retire my dad.

When I was finally able to give him that gift, it wasn't money from the NHL that did it. Instead, I had earned a windfall from a property that I'd invested in and sold with a business partner.

Real estate has been good to me over the years. The very first house I bought was a gorgeous property on the water in downtown Vancouver. A friend of mine helped me negotiate the price and connect with lenders who would help me even though I was new to the league and only making a few hundred thousand. The house was listed at $1.3 million. Twelve years and $600,000 in renovations later, I sold it for $3.6 million, not including all of the income I got every winter for renting it out to movie stars.

In between, I bought, held, and sold several other properties. The first time my real estate partner and I sold a property, the buyers paid with cash, and I suddenly had a few hundred thousand dollars on hand. I knew right away what I wanted to do. I didn't need another car or a nicer place of my own. I needed to give back to my parents. I needed to take care of them like they took care of me.

It was just a year or two into my time in the NHL, and I went to see my parents in the off-season. As usual, my visit coincided with my dad's August birthday party and barbecue. And I was cooking up a little surprise of my own.

Casually at first, I hinted at my hidden treasure: "Hey, Dad, make sure you don't burn those potatoes."

"No, not yet. They haven't been on long enough," he protested.

"Dad, I really think those potatoes need to be checked."

"They'll be fine."

"Dad, *check* the *potatoes*."

He finally stabbed at them with his fork to see they were hard as a rock and then peeled back the foil to see that they weren't actually potatoes at all. Before I went to his place, I had wrapped up $100,000 of the cash from that sale into bricks of $100 bills and covered them in foil so they looked like potatoes. Then I snuck them onto the grill before he started to make dinner.

In all my life, I had never seen him with as much as a single hundred-dollar bill in his hands. And now he had a thousand of them. With that gift and the monthly "allowance" I sent them, he never had to work another day in his life.

Dad only ever asked for one thing from me: for his birthday every year, he wanted his annual golf membership at the Salmon Arm Golf Club renewed. His retirement was filled with golf in the summer, ice fishing in the winter, and occasional monthlong stays at my home in Cabo San Lucas, Mexico. Even though he didn't have to work, if the school needed someone to fill in as a bus driver, he'd do it. He also made beautiful wood carvings with incredible skill. He was a jack-of-all-trades who lived his life to the absolute fullest. I was so honored to be able to give him that time of rest.

Standing there with handfuls of foil-covered money, he shook his head in disbelief while I tried to explain that it was my gift back to him. Through the tears that streamed down his cheeks, he said, "Who would have thought my kid could ever take care of me like this?"

That was the first time I had ever seen my dad cry.

He had coached me to become the player I needed to be. He had taught me not only how to play but how to think and how to approach life. There's no way I would have made it to the NHL without him. There's no way I'd be who I am today without him.

My first time on skates. I was just three years old.

I spent so many hours in the snow and on the outdoor rink. I was six years old living in the frozen winters of Hinton, Alberta, Canada in this picture.

My best NHL game face while wearing my Oilers colors.

That was the year we were so good we got kicked out of our league. I was eight years old and playing for the Atoms.

The Yellowhead Selects the weekend all of the greater
Vancouver area teams played—and we beat them all.

*Me skating on the Oilers ice at Northlands Coliseum, my dream come true!
I was so excited I kissed the ice when we got out there.*

*Bantam provincial champions with my friend and line mates
Jeff Holt and Jeff Connor after three overtime periods when all
of Salmon Arm, BC, showed up to watch us. We set the goal of
being provincial champions the first day of the season!*

A magical moment with my dad, Doug, and me on Shuswap Lake in Salmon Arm during a brief Winterhawk Christmas break.

The 1994 NHL draft and the legendary late Pat Quinn. I was drafted in the second round, forty-second overall in the world. My absolute dream come true.

CHAPTER FIVE

HOMEGROWN ROOKIE

✕

There's a tradition in the NHL that comes after you're called up for your rookie year. Everyone goes out for a celebratory dinner at the start of the season—the players, the trainers, and everybody—at an amazing restaurant. Mark Messier organized ours at The Forge in Miami. We had an incredible time. All the best wine. Steak and lobster. Tons of laughs and so much fun.

The thing is, it's called your rookie dinner not just because it's the first time you really get to celebrate being on an NHL team but because the rookies actually pay for it all. *For everyone. It*'s your official initiation into the NHL, and trust me: every kid who plays somewhere hopes and prays that one day they will join the club and get to buy dinner for the vets, coaches, and trainers.

When a $25,000 bill hit the table at the end of the night, it was more or less down to me and Mattias Öhlund, the first-round pick who'd gotten a much bigger contract than I had, to pick up the tab. Meanwhile, I was making something like $140,000 US and had only gotten one paycheck by then. I had a single credit card with a limit of five grand, and my cut of the bill was twice that.

But I still had to pay for it.

Everyone knew I came from nothing, and since I was still really young, they didn't give me too hard a time. Mess even covered me with his credit card. I cashed my next paychecks and gave them straight to him to pay it all back, grateful that he was so kind about it all.

The morning after the rookie dinner, everyone, including the trainers, was still feeling the effects from the night before. That's when our coach, Mike Keenan, pulled one of his out-of-the-box moves. He called a practice, knowing good and well how much we'd be hurting that next day.

My first coach in Vancouver had been a guy named Tom Renney, who was the best coach a young kid could start with in the NHL. But he got squeezed out, and Mark Messier brought in Mike Keenan—a guy with a reputation for disliking young players and being hard on them to the point of being unhinged. The two of them had won a Stanley Cup together when they were with the Rangers, and that was as far as most recommendations for him could go. Calling a practice the morning after rookie dinner, when we had days before our next game, was just the start.

Most of us were struggling to even stand up, from every single player all the way down to every member of the training staff. No one wanted to be there. But there we were, half-heartedly skating around the ice, mumbling and confused about what this guy could possibly want from us the morning after rookie dinner. We skated...and skated...and ten minutes after practice was supposed to start, Keenan finally came out and lined us up at the far end.

He looked us up and down for a minute and said, "Okay, line rushes."

The problem was, he didn't bring any pucks out. Line rushes involve three guys passing the puck between themselves while skating the length of the ice and then shooting it on the goalie, who should make the save before the next line goes. Without any pucks, we were just...lines. There was nothing to rush. Naturally, everyone hesitated. But Keenan was undeterred.

"Go!" he yelled. We all kind of looked around at each other before the first line took off, not really knowing what they were supposed to do. Still, Keenan was yelling: "Snap it around, boys!"

Now we were all laughing—and slowly getting into it. One guy reluctantly made a pretend pass to the other, who whipped a pretend pass to another, and then the goalie dove to block the pretend shot.

On we went, with future Hall of Famers like Messier, Bure, Linden, and Mogilny diving and slapping at the nothing on the ice, goalies making fake double pad saves, some of us celebrating fake goals, and everyone trying not to be too obvious with our "this guy is crazy" glances at each other. We were all laughing hysterically as we started having fun with it, and the fake plays became more and more dramatic.

Fifteen minutes later, he was satisfied, and the practice was over. Looking back, I am sure he wanted to get us out of bed and sweat some booze out before resting for a couple of days. Without any pucks on the ice, we couldn't kill each other in our hungover stupor.

I never saw another practice without pucks in the NHL or ever again in my life. If it made any sense at all, no one else was doing it. But I'm writing this with a huge smile on my face, because it was another crazy day in the NHL that I will never forget. It set the tone for my rookie year and the unpredictable coach who would get me through it.

///

Mike Keenan was hot and cold in every aspect of his career. He'd either love you or hate you, and if you were a young player, your odds of being on the good side of that equation were low. Messier liked me, though, so that gave me a little bit of a grace period. Keenan couldn't hate me outright. But I had to show him something to keep that going.

During one of the first few games Keenan was coaching with his new team, the first period of a game went by without me getting to play. Second period, I watched and waited for him to call my line, and then I felt this stab in my kidneys, just above the hockey pants where the shoulder pads leave a gap when you sit down. I flinched and looked around to see Keenan standing behind me, sneering and tapping his toes on the ground.

I was still terrified of losing my job—I could be sent down and buried in the minors at any time if Keenan didn't like me. This unpredictable coach essentially held my life in his hands, which is not the ideal condition to be playing your best hockey. But I wasn't going to be denied. I weighed my options and then turned back around to watch the game and wait for my shift. Then I felt it again. An unmistakable dress-shoe kick to the kidney.

I flipped around and snapped, "What is your problem, man?"

He snapped right back with, "What have you done out there today? I don't even know who you are. You haven't done anything tonight! Why should I even keep you around?"

Seriously? I asked him how I was supposed to do anything when he hadn't given me a shift, and he kept prodding about sending me home if I wasn't going to do something.

"Put me on the ice. I'll show you something."

So he did. And I did.

He threw me out on left wing when my normal position was center ice or right wing, no doubt trying to throw me off balance even more. I immediately spotted the right wing for the other team and told him it was time to go. Thankfully, I had a willing combatant. We dropped gloves, and I went after him hard. Caught him with a couple of punches early that dropped him to his knees. And as soon as I knew I had him, I looked up at the bench. Keenan was watching me. *Good.*

I pounded the kid onto the ice, punching over and over like I was starting a lawnmower on his face, all while staring right into Keenan's eyes. I wasn't even looking down at the kid. As the refs pulled me off, I kept staring. I made them push me backward to the penalty box, but I never broke eye contact with Keenan.

I stared as long as I could, sending a clear *don't ever fucking challenge me again* message.

And he stared back, until about halfway across the ice, when a huge grin broke out across his face. He could push my buttons and get exactly what he wanted, and he loved it. I became his new project. He could wind me up and let me go, and I would do what had to be done. I was becoming the gladiator. Someone who could bang or crash or fight every night and chip in with the odd goal now and then. He knew he could get an energetic eight to ten minutes from me every night, so that's what I did. If I could make an impact every time, I knew it would keep me in the game.

///

With Keenan, "hot and cold" really meant unpredictable and sometimes dangerous. Once, after the second period had ended on a low note, he came into the locker room raging. He grabbed a goalie stick from Artūrs Irbe and started smashing it against the wall as he yelled.

If you aren't familiar with the size and density of a goalie stick, this is a pretty impressive feat. It also comes with a lot of cracking, splintering, and shattering—not just a clean break in two.

Maybe he was trying to get us fired up, but it just looked like losing his mind. When he got it down to shards, he threw what was left of the stick toward the whiteboard at the front of the room. Unfortunately, his timing was off and the release came too late. The thing started to spin like a boomerang through the air, flipping end over end until it landed...across my wrists.

I had been sitting by the whiteboard, Alexander Mogilny on one side of me and Brian Noonan on the other side, leaning onto my hands and trying not to make eye contact with him when he threw that thing. Thank God for wrist guards because when it hit, it shattered. The biggest piece that flew off of my wrists and forearms flew into the drywall at the front of the room and dented the wall.

We were stunned. Noonan screamed at him to calm the fuck down before he killed somebody, and he must have known he'd crossed a line too. He literally ran out of the room.

We were all dumbfounded. He'd lost his mind, nearly killed someone, and took off in a sprint. He had obviously been trying to motivate us, but it wasn't enough. We lost the game, and the next day I had to figure out how to handle my coach nearly injuring me and others between periods.

The consensus from the guys was that I had to confront him in some way. Storm into his office? Scream right back at him? Take a more measured or serious approach? And honestly, I didn't want to piss that kind of a guy off, or I was sure I'd get sent back down.

After thinking about it all night, it came to me. I could do the exact opposite of what everyone expected and still make my point. So before practice and earlier than our ten thirty meeting, I went into the dressing room and found all of the goalie equipment, including Artūr's famous goalie mask. Then I told all the guys to put their helmets on before the meeting started. Just in case.

When Keenan walked into the room for the meeting, he found a room full of guys in their underwear with their helmets on, and me in full goalie gear sitting back in my stall. If he was going to lose it again, we were prepared. The guys thought it was hilarious, and I thought it made my point.

Funny thing, though, Keenan had the exact same idea.

He came walking into the dressing room holding the front end of a stretcher with one of our trainers bringing up the rear.

Just in case.

///

For all of his flaws, you had to give Mike credit for his creativity. He was a master trickster who would just pop up out of nowhere. Sometimes he would be face-down in the trainer's room getting a massage or hidden in the corner of the steam room. You always had to have your radar on and be careful what you said. A toilet stall, the hot tub—there was no escaping the guy.

Once, he gave a bellman a big goalie stick to have signed after a road game in Chicago. But because our team lost, Keenan set a midnight curfew for the entire team, and he asked the bellman to only get autographs from guys coming in after that.

The next day, he walked into the dressing room before practice holding this goalie sick like a smoking gun. The guilty parties knew they'd been caught, and we couldn't help but laugh as they made the long walk to the coach's office for a "private" meeting.

It was creative, resourceful, and hilarious all at the same time.

But at some point in that first year, Keenan found out I was rooming with Mattias and pulled us into his office.

"You don't think I know what you guys do every day?"

We looked at each other, a little bit confused and a whole lot worried that we were going to get in trouble or sent down. He kept on:

"There's not one thing that you do in this city that I don't know about. Nothing. People tell me stuff...but as long as you keep playing great, I don't care. But don't ever think you're getting away with stuff. I know, and the whole city knows."

That was it. He just had to flex that control on us a little bit. And it wasn't just us. One morning we pulled into the parking lot under the building for practice, only to find that everyone else's cars were already there.

We ran into the Coliseum, checking our watches and trying to figure out what went wrong. In the changing room, everyone's "underwear," the clothes they wear under their gear, was already gone. Something had obviously gone wrong, and we were sure we were going to get in trouble for it. In the training room, we found Mike Bernstein and asked him what was going on.

"Everyone's in the workout room. You should go say hi."

That was going to be it. If we missed a workout or a weigh-in or a team stretch, the consequences wouldn't be pretty.

We ran into the workout room thinking we were late for something that we must have forgotten about or missed out on. Inside, everyone else on the team—which, since Mattias and I were the rookies, meant they were long-time veterans—was drenched in sweat and lined up on the stationary bikes pedaling away in the middle of a tough bike workout. Glaring at us. And then Keenan came. There was no telling what he might do to teach a couple of rookies a lesson.

Instead, Keenan made much more of a spectacle by greeting us with smiles and pride. "Oh, there's my boys! Look at these guys. This is what fitness looks like, right here." Then he turned his attention to the room and continued, "These two young fuckwads are in better shape than all *you* fat fucks put together!" This was obviously not the case, comparing two rookies to a room full of professional athletes playing in the best league in the world. He just wanted to create some chaos. And he did.

Everyone in the room wanted to kill us, except Keenan, who went on celebrating us and using us as justification for putting them through the wringer.

Keenan always wanted things to be a little bit off balance. Random outbursts or meetings or articles in the paper, or a trade out of the blue would pop up at the strangest times for as long as I knew him. All in all, I think he and I came to an understanding. He pushed me, but when I pushed back, he loved it. He knew he could fire me up and that I wouldn't back down or wither away. The players who would shrink or disappear when challenged did not last with him. He helped me break into the league, and I believe he respected me in the end.

For all of his quirks, Keenan was an excellent coach and ran a great bench. When things were going great, sometimes he would cancel practice on the road and take the entire team to the spa. When it wasn't going well, practices (and life) were miserable.

Right or wrong, he had a Stanley Cup ring on his resume, and I was grateful he let me stay on the team and learn how to become a better pro.

///

Mattias and I lived in a small townhouse down on the sea wall, and then we both decided to move to a penthouse down by Stanley Park. It was a gorgeous place with views of the ocean, all kinds of biking trails, and little regional float planes always taking off on the inlet going in and out of the city. To park, you had to drive down into what we called the bat cave. There was a computer screen you'd punch some numbers in, and the car would be automatically lowered down onto tracks in this high-tech elevator system that pulled it into a parking place. When you needed it back, you'd punch the screen and call it back up. Everything about that place was high-tech, computer-chipped, and super secure. Plus, there were only four people staying in that entire five-story building, and we were two of them. That didn't prevent drama from finding us anyway.

One day we were on the way to a game when Mattias crashed his brand-new Jaguar into a police car. Another night—or early morning, actually, around three after a road trip—we stowed Mattias's car in the bat cave and took all our bags in to put them away...when someone rang the buzzer to the penthouse. In high-tech fashion, an image of that person came up on the computer screen in our entryway. We had no idea who he was. He looked like he was of Asian descent of some sort, but he wasn't Stanley Ho, the casino owner who we were renting from. He held what looked like a rake and had a bandana on his head, so I thought he must be there to do some work.

I buzzed back, "Can we help you?"

"Let me in."

Gardener, maybe?

"It's three in the morning. What company are you with? What do you need?"

"Let me in the house or I'll kill you."

"Uh...Ohlie?" I looked at Mattias—he was as confused as me.

With both of us looking closely at the screen and trying to stall the guy, we realized it wasn't a rake in his hand at all. It was a giant samurai sword. And it was definitely real.

The guy lost it. He couldn't get directly in without the fob or our approval, but he had a fucking samurai sword. So he started slicing away at the wraps on the doors and anything he could find that might cut away, the whole time screaming that he was going to kill us.

We called NHL security, Keith Hammond, to see what we should do, and he called the cops. When the cops screeched up to the house with lights and sirens blazing, the crazy guy took off, leading a high-speed chase through the streets of Vancouver. Before we knew it, it was four in the morning, and cops were hanging out in our kitchen. I think they liked hanging out with a couple of Canucks, so they weren't in any real rush to leave. I guess the psychopath could have come back. They were saying things like, "This is a legitimate threat," and "We have to stay on watch," but we just wanted to crash after the crazy long day.

After a high-speed chase, the involvement of a SWAT team, and all kinds of TV coverage, they finally caught the guy. He was convinced that Stanley Ho owed him money and that he was going to get to him through us. Somehow.

Not surprisingly, the cops later told us the man had been on meth.

He did not get his money that night, and we did not get sleep. But we did get a great story to tell the guys a few hours later at practice.

After a year of that kind of drama and fun, our time as single rookies enjoying downtown Vancouver ended when Mattias invited a beautiful Swedish girl named Linda to come visit. He said she wouldn't stay too long, but the stacks of suitcases she brought with her said otherwise.[14] When they moved out, Peter Schaefer moved in to room with me.

Peter's one of the nicest guys you'll ever meet—a rookie at the time, but I knew him from juniors as a kid out of the East who was lighting the whole league up. He was the one who hooked me up with that tiny place of his uncle's when I moved to Vancouver. Just a couple of years after I was crunching into that tiny basement bathroom, we were rooming together and having the best of times. Like Mattias, Peter and I got as close as brothers. Over the years, we vacationed together, were in each other's weddings, and even had kids born on the same day, calling each other from the delivery rooms.

I don't think all teammates and roommates are lucky enough to have that kind of bond. I'm forever grateful that my experience in the NHL left me with brothers for life.

///

---

14 Linda was awesome, and we were all roommates for a while before they wanted to get their own place. Twenty years later, Mattias and Linda are still married today, with two beautiful children together.

My salary was low by NHL standards, but it let me do things that I would never have been able to do otherwise. Since I didn't know how to cook, me and the guys were out every night eating in Vancouver's amazing restaurants and hanging out with locals. I still had friends going to the University of British Columbia, so I'd hang out there on my days off. I would buy the whole bar twenty-five-cent shots and feel like such a big deal. It was hilarious.

Vancouver *made me* feel like a big deal. The vibe there was incredible. All of my friends and family were nearby, and the fans loved me. After all, I was a local guy who made it from nothing. I was every hockey fan's dream come true.

Just last year, my kids were shocked when I got pulled over in Vancouver and the cop recognized my name from my ID. "Dave Scatchard the hockey player?" Twenty years had passed since I played there, but he told me how much he loved my play and sent me off without so much as a warning. Canada loves its players, and I was truly one of their own. I'm truly grateful for my time in Vancouver—for the amazing fans and for the lifelong friends I made during my time there. But for all of that love for the Canucks, I ran into a brick wall that would change everything for me.

A brick wall by the name of Marc Crawford.

CHAPTER SIX

GOLDEN YEARS ON THE ISLAND

Keenan might have been a guy you love to hate, but his replacement on the Canucks was one you just hated. I didn't know anyone who liked the guy, and he didn't seem to like anyone either, from the doorman and the security guards to us.

Marc Crawford had just led Colorado to a Stanley Cup, but inexplicably, that team had also let him go. That told a bunch of us that he had an all-star team that anyone could have taken to the Cup. It didn't matter. He showed up with a chip on his shoulder and a list of guys he wanted off the team just because we were young, without even seeing us play. There was no warming up to this guy.

As soon as I came to terms with my new reality, I started conversations about trades. I wanted to spend the Christmas holiday with my friends and family before moving on to a team with better opportunities and, if I'm totally honest, a better coach—one who would see my value and want to give me an opportunity to play. Since the NHL freezes rosters two days before Christmas anyway, I thought that request was a safe bet, and I settled in to enjoy the festivities.

Four days before Christmas, the team got together for a holiday party at Ed Jovanovski's house, hanging out and having a great time. It was a few years before any of us had cell phones, so when the phone rang in the room downstairs where we were playing pool, it could have been for anybody. But it was the GM Brian Burke from the Canucks asking to speak to me.

He wanted to tell me how pivotal I was in the trade deal they had just made and how he thought it would be a good move for my career—a move that was not only happening before Christmas but was taking me to the Islanders.

The league-owned Islanders.

The league-owned Islanders that had just lost their owner to jail time for buying the team with no money.

The Islanders that had no money. The Islanders that couldn't win.

He delivered the blow before I knew what hit me and asked me to pass the phone to our goalie, Kevin Weekes.

The whole party atmosphere was crashing down around those of us next to the phone. Schaefs (Peter Schaefer) was upset about losing me as his roommate, and we had a quick cry out on the patio. Weekes was taking his own news hard, and Bill Muckalt was trying to comfort him with back pats and "it's okay, big guy" reassurances. Then Weekes pulled the whole party to a stop, as if a record scratched everything into silence: "Mucky, phone's for you."

We went from a bunch of guys having a great time to a bunch of guys crying and consoling each other in just a few minutes. All three of us were going together, at ten the next morning. With a game to play the day after that. At least, on what we hoped was the bright side, we would spend Christmas in New York.

Except none of us knew anyone in New York, and we would quickly find out that no one there knew us either.

///

eaving Vancouver was a whirlwind. We went directly home from the party and started gathering our things, trying to fit enough to get us through the rest of the season in just a couple of bags. Loaded down with as much as we could carry, we waded through fans and media to get to the plane.

There were video cameras, interviews, and people sending us off. After our almost five-hour flight to New York, Weekesy— the guy who was always dressed immaculately—told us we needed to make a good impression when we landed and found a similar crowd waiting for us. So, taking turns crammed into the bathroom to change on the plane, we all put on suits and did our hair while we tried to figure out what New York was going to be like.

On the ground, we gathered up our stuff from baggage claim and headed out into the chilly New York air, expecting the onslaught of cameras and attention...but no one was there. At all.

No media. No fans. Not even a team representative to tell us what to do. We had no idea where we were staying or how to get there. Even worse, after multiple calls with no answer, we were finally able to get ahold of the GM, Mike Milbury, to figure out what was going on. His "oh, shit" reaction didn't give us much hope.

He had us grab a stretch limo—for three big hockey guys and all of our belongings and gear—and told us to bring him the receipt to reimburse us later.

It was like something out of a movie, but a *Bad News Bears* type of comedy more than an inspirational sports flick.

We called a company from the airport that showed up with a shitty stretch limo—white, of course. We stared at it, then each other, and then got to work. After the trunk was filled with suitcases and backpacks, we opened up all the doors to fit Weeksey's goalie pads and sticks and then our equipment and sticks. Two-thirds of the thing was filled up, with the three of us crammed onto the bench seat in the back. Then we took it through a McDonald's drive-through and ordered everything we could before we got back to the hotel.

That Long Island Marriot would become home for the next five months—that is, after I changed rooms a half dozen times trying to find a mattress that wasn't warped or soft. Forget Christmas in New York. This was life on the Island, and there was nothing more to do except play and train. And damn if our team didn't need that.

The Islanders were a team of tradition, a former Dynasty that won four Cups in a row in the eighties but was now owned by the league after an embarrassing situation where a guy named Spano conned the entire league and somehow bought the team with no money.[15] So we were young and broke, just like I'd been a few years before. Our budget ran at about a third of the league average. We were all trying to establish ourselves in the league individually, but the team was in shambles.

Milbury pulled me aside, once we finally got to meet him, and told me how excited he was to have me. They thought I had a real future there, but not that season. It was barely Christmas, and the team was already mathematically eliminated from the playoffs. There was nothing left to shoot for.

It wasn't ideal news, but it gave us a green light to explore the city for the rest of the season. Our one goal was to play hard in every game, so we decided we would take a (much nicer) limo into Manhattan when we won games, and we'd stay on the Island if we lost. That became our motivation to win, which became our motivation to pull together, at least a little bit.

It was...something, anyway. It was nothing like the tight ship Vancouver ran, but with no owner, no fans showing up at the games, no incentive to get people to sign with us as free agents, no clear path out of the pit, what else could they do?

Bad habits and routines were starting take over a team that had no real leadership presence. In my very first game with the

---

15 Kevin Connolly, who I got to know during Rick Dipietro's wedding, did a great documentary on it, called *Big Shot*. He was a super nice guy and huge Islander fan.

Islanders, it was obvious that we were going to lose. I was so angry, I felt like I needed to send a message. Just like I had in Vancouver, I lined up against my opponent after being down a few goals with less than ten minutes left to go in the game and asked him to fight. He was up for it, and I got the best of him—sending a message to my team that we would no longer go down without a fight.

Things were going to have to change. I wasn't going to allow losing to be acceptable or habitual anymore.

We had a young team of single guys with no responsibilities, so dinner and drinks after most games were all we had to do in Long Island. Because we didn't have our own plane like most teams in the league, we stayed over in most cities instead of flying home. That meant that there weren't often practices the next morning to stand as consequences.[16] We even flew commercial to games, crammed into too-small seats next to little old ladies and navigating layovers and late nights to eventually make our way home.

Routine can make or break your night, your season, your career. I was always one of the first guys at the rink, two or three hours before a game would start. Once while in Vancouver, Glen Hanlon walked in and caught me squatting 375 pounds on the bar, and he lost it. "What the fuck are you doing? We've got a game!"

"I know, Hanny. I've just got extra energy today that I want to get out before the game."

---

16 We did get to spend time with our head coach and four-time Cup winner Butch Goring on those nights. I could listen to him tell stories about that Islander dynasty for hours.

He couldn't fathom how that could be true, but it was. Later in my career, I learned to control those nerves more effectively. But without working those nerves out throwing weight around, sprinting, or riding the bike, I'd vibrate a little bit too high. I might take a pointless penalty, overcheck, or lose some control.

When you've got that routine, that energy coming from more than one player, the line starts to come together. The best year I ever had was when Jason Blake and I would do our warm-ups together. At the end of our routine, I'd wrap him up and pop his back, and then he'd do the same for me. Then we'd high-five and head out. That was how we started every single game.

The combination of youth and a disciplined routine could get explosive. That kind of energy before and during a game can carry you through almost anything. I could come into the building barely able to walk or feeling like trash from the flu and still be able to find the zone.

It took some time to get the team on their feet, especially since the low budget meant guys were always being rotated out from the minors. But once we found our groove, it was some of the best hockey of my life.

///

My first hat trick in the NHL happened on the Islanders. You get plenty of them as a kid, but in the league, a lot has to come together to make it work. When you're on the third line with limited ice time, it's even more challenging.

By then, we were the top-scoring third line in the NHL. That game, Jason Blake and Jason Weimer were working their butts off to get the puck to me in the slot.[17] The first one went in early, and then a second shot ripped home.

The next time out, they brought out some tough guys against us, and one of them skated up to me ready to fight.

I didn't often say no to a fight, but I was on a mission.

He said, "Scatch, you wanna go?"

"I'm not fighting you tonight, man. I'm gonna go get my hat trick."

He countered back to get in my head: "You'll never have a hat trick in this league."

I laughed. "Just watch."

Nothing could get me off my game. I was looking for open ice and a line to the net. When it happened, it seemed so fast. *Bang, bang.* Then Weemes was handing me the puck, and hats were littering the ice, and I had my first hat trick in the NHL. When it was over and I was announced as the first star of the game, I picked up a sombrero that someone had thrown on the ice and wore it as I skated around, saluting the Long Island faithful.

I don't even remember the motions that scored the goal. It felt like a dream in flow state, with no stress or weight or pressure. I could have been slashed or cross-checked in front of the net, but my only concern was doing my thing. The thing I'd done tens of thousands of times in the basement, the backyard, the practices, and the visualizations.

In that moment, it didn't even feel like work. It was just what my body knew how to do. I was floating.

---

17 Yeah, the same Jason Weimer whose dad was my coach in Kimberley and the same Jason Weimer who was on the Winterhawks with me.

It's something we were able to cultivate on the Islanders. Both my wingers and I would get on the same page, pushing each other to get into the zone before and during games. We'd push for that synergy that can move a team like they're one unit. We'd push ourselves in practices because the more intensity you go through together, the more you're forged together into one fluid machine. And when you're there, *everything* gets to be fun.

It was fun for us, anyway.

Midway into the second full year with the Islanders, I was doing great. My career had jumped up to where I always thought it could be. Crawford was still coaching the Canucks, and there's no way I could have done so well on his team.

I didn't see him again until the Canucks came into Long Island needing a big win. My first shift was right next to their bench. Oddly, I noticed someone yelling at me from that direction, but in a high pitch that didn't sound at all like a player. When I caught something like, "I've got lots of guys for you..." I looked over to see Crawford red-faced and screaming.

To be honest, he hadn't crossed my mind before then. I was enjoying playing the game against some of my old friends. I yelled back, "If you need to send somebody out here to do your work, go ahead," and kept on with my game.

He kept on screaming at me every chance he got, and I kept playing my game until the last minutes when I set my teammate up for the game-winning goal. We pulled out the win, and I skated by their bench one more time to rub it in his face just a little and then head off to the dressing room.

After high fives and congratulations, I took off all my equipment and jersey and hung it up in my stall in the Islander dressing room, ready to end the night, when our tough guy Eric Cairns came running into the dressing room. "You've got to see this, Scatch. Crawford is out in the hallway—he wants to fight you."

Underneath Nassau Coliseum, there's a tunnel that connects the two dressing rooms. In the middle of the tunnel, there's a big accordion screen that keeps the two teams separate thanks to a fight Eric Cairns had once with Matthew Barnaby after they got kicked out of a game—for fighting, of course. After Crawford screamed at me for three hours, I was hoping he'd found a way through the screen.

Instead, I found him pressed up against it, spitting and yelling and calling me names, while my whole team and I laughed at him from the other side.

The next morning, Mike Milbury called me into his office to ask what had happened. "I got a call from Burkie, and Crawford told him you were causing stuff on the ice last night and that you challenged him to fight. I don't know what happened, but you need to call Brian Burke and fix it."

I called Burkie, who was now back in Vancouver, and their team had a day off. Sure enough, Burkie had heard that I had screamed at Crawford the whole game and then went after him to fight him.

"Brian, you know I'm an honest guy, right?"

"Yeah, that's what I love about you."

"He's lying out of his ass. Go ask every person on your team's bench what happened, and they'll back me up. They were rolling their eyes at him the whole night."

"Scatch, do you swear that's what happened? I don't want any of my coaches ever yelling at a player on the ice. If that's how it really went down...I give you 100 percent free rein to grab that guy and beat the shit out of him any time you ever see him. You have my blessing."

And that was it for me and Crawford—though he had some heftier consequences coming his way later. Eventually, he was suspended from the Blackhawks for conduct unbecoming of a coach. Maybe this time he'd finally learned his lesson.

But probably not.

///

Consequences look different in every organization, but perhaps the most bizarre came after the first period of a game against the Tampa Bay Lightning. Five of us were called into the coach's room, which isn't usually a good sign. We expected them to ask us to start a line brawl or do something crazy to get the team involved, especially since we were all tough guys.

When we got there, the coach was with Mike Milbury, who explained what was going on. He said, "You five are the only ones trying out there. Everyone else has screwed the pooch. So I want you to go out there and start the period, and then stay out there. Don't change. Don't even look at the bench. It could be a few minutes, but don't worry about it. Just keep going."

Hockey is a game of quick bursts of huge amounts of energy. We don't stick around forever like in basketball or soccer—a forty-five-second shift is starting to get long. A couple of minutes would be brutal. Milbury explained, "We want to send the other guys a message. If they're not going to play, then they don't get to play at all. Rest between whistles. You'll know when it's time."

The first shift happened pretty fast end to end, with Tampa's superstar Vinny LeCavalier starting the period against me and my line. When the whistle went and they changed but we didn't, there was immediate confusion on both benches. Then the ref dropped the puck again, and it was back and forth for a shorter whistle, and we took the chance to catch our breath. Third whistle, we had regained some energy to run a longer shift. Then we got smart about it and started sending one guy in on the forecheck in the offensive zone while three or four hung back to rest.

Four minutes in, one of us got tired and took a penalty. We thought that would definitely trigger a switch, but nothing happened. The face-off happened next to Tampa's bench, and we could hear them laughing about it. LeCavalier came out and asked what was going on. I shrugged and told him to keep watching.

The cool thing about killing a penalty is you get to shoot the puck all the way down the ice without chasing it down. You wait for them to come to you and then play a team zone defense. It turned into a longer break that let us catch our breath.

Meanwhile, all these superstars making millions a year were just stuck on the bench without getting to play at all. For six and a half or seven minutes—something like a third of a period—they never touched the ice. The Lightning players were cracking up, watching guys like Steve Webb try to catch their breath between whistles. Our team was pissed. I was having a blast with all this ice time and this unique situation, but the guys on the bench weren't happy.

We scored once the normal rotation picked up again, but we still lost the game. Whether or not it taught a lesson is up for debate, but I don't think any of us have forgotten it.

///

Everyone is motivated by something, and me and Mariusz Czerkawski, one of my favorite teammates to play with, found something fun to keep us going. The guy loved life. He had a ton of skill, loved the lifestyle, and enjoyed good food and beautiful clothes. During the all-star break, we decided on a whim to go down to South Beach, Miami. The vibe was amazing. We had a ton of fun. And then...we came back to a struggling team.

That year, I wanted to hit twenty goals, and there was a bonus waiting for me if I hit it. Mariusz had one coming too, so to stay motivated even when the whole team wasn't quite there yet, we decided to set another goal. If we both hit our bonuses, we would take a huge chunk of our money down to South Beach after the season ended to celebrate with it.

We picked code words—he would say *NB* to me for Nikki Beach, a day club that people would come to wearing swimsuits and hanging out until it turned into a night club once the sun went down. I'd respond with *SB* for South Beach, and we'd use that to get pumped up before games. It was a challenge for us both, but we'd promised each other, and we worked hard at it the rest of the year.

With two or three games left in the season, I scored my twentieth against Garth Snow, who later became a teammate and ultimately the GM of the Islanders, to reach my bonus. For Mariusz, it came down to the last game. He needed two goals to hit his bonus, and the coaching staff wasn't doing him any favors.

I can still hear him on the bench, watching for his opportunity, mumbling in his deep voice and thick Polish accent,

"Hey, boss, you know, maybe, like, we get the two goals and the bonus, you know. Maybe we go down to South Beach. Maybe spend our bonuses on amazing dinners, get the limos and the suites, champagne, strawberries, and sun. Is nice!"

So when he told me, "Give me puck. I need my two goals today, okay?" I did all I could to help.

After scoring a goal early in the game, he just needed one more to get his bonus. Every player on our team did whatever he could to help Chow get it. His wingers on other lines short-shifted, trying to get him on the ice more, and we all fed him the puck every chance we had. The game was close, and it came down to the last minutes. We started coaching ourselves, telling the other wingers to go out for just a few seconds to get Chow back on the ice.

I'll be damned if he didn't score the goal and then throw his gloves off like we'd just won the Stanley Cup. The whole bench erupted with him, like it was the greatest game we'd ever played.

The fans were understandably confused. We celebrated more then than when Chow hit a third and we managed to win 3–2. The win wasn't enough to get us into the playoffs, but we found serious joy in it anyway, even if no one else knew why.

After the year-end meetings closed up a rough season, Mariusz and I made good on our deal. We flew down to South Beach with a few other guys and headed right to Nikki Beach like we'd envisioned. We didn't actually take our whole bonuses, but we both had pockets full of cash ready to party with.

I peeled off a couple hundred from my stack and gave them to the bouncer. "I know it's early, but we want to get this taken care of now. Can you make sure we're safe and having fun at the best table tonight? Make sure we don't do anything stupid?" Then word got out to the manager, who came to check on us, and we doubled down. "We're celebrating a good season, so we want this to be the most special table of the night. We're not afraid to invest in it."

As the sun started to go down, Chow chimed in. "Hey, boss. We need like-a four of the magnums of Cristal, you know. Maybe like twenty-five glasses. Some strawberries, maybe some chocolates for the ladies. You know, nice."

We were ready.

Twenty-some seats.

Four or five guys.

Tables full of champagne and wine and desserts.

And we waited.

It was like bees to honey. For hours and hours, we had the time of our lives. Our table was the best one in the room. We laughed our heads off, dancing and joking and having the best night—at some point, I even ran into Jamie Foxx and hung out with him for a little bit.

Somewhere around midnight, I took off to the bathroom for a quick second...and as I made my way back to the table it was like a record scratched. I walked up to our table, completely confused—the girls were gone, the party was gone, and the entire vibe had changed. Waiters were even moving our tables.

Chow was looking at me, wide-eyed. "Boss, I don't say nothing! I don't say nothing. Where did everyone go?"

We tried to find management to ask what had happened when an entourage of dozens of people and security guards came pouring in, with newly renamed P. Diddy at the center. We watched, jaws dropped, as the entire room gravitated toward the tables that had been ours. We'd basically pre-gamed his entire night for him.

One guy from his crew came over and surprised me. "P. Diddy wants to talk to you."

I slowly made my way over to P. Diddy's table, and he said, "Hey, man, I just want to apologize. I love how you guys are hanging. You're more than welcome to join us—we don't want to steal the whole party."

My ego answered before I could: "We're good."

Chow and I and our buddies finished the night on our own. This coal-mining kid and his friends who all grew up with nothing already had had the best night of our lives partying with supermodels and movie stars in Miami without checking prices or worrying about a thing.

For one night, we got to turn down one of the biggest stars of our time. We let ourselves celebrate instead of putting our heads down for next year or looking back in regret over the previous year. We enjoyed our hard work, and we achieved our goal. And we stopped to celebrate before moving on. And that just made us want to work harder the next time so we could party even harder when the time came. Who knows? Maybe P. Diddy would even pre-game for us.[18]

---

18 Yeah, no, that was never going to happen.

CHAPTER SEVEN

A LIFE WITHOUT LIMITS

The company I kept changed completely once the Islanders started to take off. We were an establishment of New York City, and we were starting to do the fans right. Long Island loved us; Manhattan was our playground, and I found myself in surreal situations time and time again.

But not all the pieces of being an athlete were fun and games. Especially in New York in 2001.

Everyone remembers where they were on September 11. For me, it was eating breakfast at a restaurant in a hotel in Lake Placid, New York, during training camp with the Islanders. I walked downstairs to see TVs all turned to the smoke pouring out of the first tower. The morning casually carried on with uncertainty about what had actually happened until the second plane struck. The whole room gasped, and nothing would ever be the same.

It took a few extra days to wrap up training camp, but as soon as we got back to Long Island, the entire Islander team and trainers went down to ground zero. Naively, we thought that we could support the first responders in some way. Maybe boost their morale, since a lot of the firefighters serving there were from Long Island. But whatever we thought we were going to give them by going down there, we were wrong.

The look of defeat on their faces...I won't ever be able to describe it.

Of course, they weren't happy to see the New York Islanders. *Of course*, we couldn't make their day. It looked like they'd all seen—what, a ghost? No, man. Their whole world was ghosts now. There was just a deep, inconsolable sadness about what they had to do.

With millions of pounds of concrete all piled in on itself, how were they supposed to find anybody? They'd lost brothers and sisters, teammates, neighbors, and friends, and there was no sign of life in the rubble. And still they kept on. It was like seeing soldiers in a losing battle still pressing on. Something about who they were—who they really were at their core— meant they couldn't give up hope of a miracle.

Everyone we met was covered head to toe in soot and dust. The rubber on the soles of our shoes started to melt from the fires still burning down underneath us all. And still those first responders kept going. Kept digging. Kept trying. Seventy-two hours at a time, around the clock, with no reward. Many of those who survived would go on to get cancer and lung disease. Those who didn't make it out would never be forgotten. After that day, we stopped trying to make them happy and started doing all we could to honor them.

A month later, the Concert for New York City benefit came together to honor those first responders and raise money for charities still working for the families. Every celebrity and musician you could think of turned out to perform, donate, and show their support. The Who, David Bowie, Elton John, Eric Clapton, Mick Jagger, Keith Richards, Bon Jovi, Jay-Z, Destiny's Child, Backstreet Boys, James Taylor, Billy Joel, Melissa Etheridge, Kid Rock, Adam Sandler...and me and Michael Peca, our team captain.

And every sports team in the surrounding area picked two athletes to participate.

I hung out with Susan Sarandon. I ran into Harrison Ford in the bathroom. From my seat, Sheryl Crow was in my line of view. Natalie Portman was right next to me. Whatever had happened to the world, it was completely upside down. None of it felt real. Just wrapped up in emotions and importance. It didn't even matter that we were surrounded by celebrities—the first responders and their families on the floor of Madison Square Garden were all any of us cared about.

Because of them, because of the celebrities, because of the broadcast and the seriousness and the weight of it all, my twenty seconds on stage were terrifying.

The whole country felt the loss of that tragedy, but not like New York.

Thousands of incredible people around me and hundreds of millions were watching on TV, and I couldn't remember my one line. None of the other athletes were perfect at the mic either, but it didn't seem like they were as scared as I was. I said something quick and from the heart and then hurried off stage. It was the biggest thing I ever had the opportunity to do, and I was so grateful for it.

The first game back, a huge American flag covered the whole surface of the arena. I remember skating out wearing an FDNY hat while the iconic emcee Michael Buffer announced us all. Both teams waved the same flag and cheered for the same broken city. We were all there together, grieving the same loss.

And together, we found our way back to better, brighter days.

///

Some time that fall, out in Santa Monica, the hotel phone light flashed a message after our game against LA. Charles Wang, owner of Computer Associates, had purchased the team, taken over, and invested in some players to help us get to the next level. We had a ton of talent on the ice and a ton of fun off of it.

Brad Isbister, my old Portland Winterhawks teammate, and I were roommates at home and on the road,[19] and we thought we were in for the night. Coaches had set a curfew of eleven for some reason, even though our next game wasn't for a couple of days—but the message was from a guy named Chief.

---

19 We ended up played together in juniors with the Winterhawks and then with the Islanders and also ended up on the Bruins together.

Hey, Dave. I'm a big Islander fan, and I wanted to let you know I am the road manager for this band called Nickelback. They're opening up for Fuel tonight at Whiskey A Go Go in LA. We'd love to take care of any of the guys who want to come down and watch the show. We'll buy them some beers. It'll be fun!

None of us knew who Nickelback was, but we started making calls anyway. Probably half the team wanted to go, so we piled into cabs and headed out to the ten o'clock show. Forget the curfew, man. We made an executive decision that since we didn't play for two days, it was worth the risk of pissing the coach off—and there was strength in numbers.

Chief was clearly the man in charge, mixing soundboards and managing them on the road. He came out with a few buckets of Coronas for the dozen of us spread out around this little venue. Their big hit "How You Remind Me" had just come out, and they were killing it in the small venues they'd booked before they started to take off.

After Fuel finished up, Nickelback's lead singer Chad came out to find us and invited us onto their bus. If you're keeping track, that's one bus for the band, crew, and twelve great big hockey guys. It was never going to last, so someone mentioned going out.

Just across the street, there was the Rainbow Bar and Grill, an after-hours venue where all kinds of celebrities and rock stars famously hung out. It didn't disappoint. Guys from Poison were there, guys from the Rolling Stones...and then us rolling in with a brand-new band and half of a hockey team.

Usually, when we went places, we were the guys who would be sharing all of the stories. This time we got to be the fans, like little kids listening in awe to our idols. Poison's CC Deville was holding court, and his stories would make your head spin if your jaw wasn't already on the floor.

And just like rebellious kids, we had to sneak in hours past curfew without getting caught.

Pulling back up to the hotel in our caravan of cabs around two thirty, we could see through the hotel lobby doors to our impending doom. Assistant coach Crow (Greg Cronin) was sitting in the inner courtyard, waiting to bust anyone out late. The first guys who saw him started trying to signal to the others, reaching out of the windows and waving all the cabs around to the back of the hotel to see if we could get in without Crow noticing us. We snuck into the service entrance and took a back elevator up to our floors, which circled around the courtyard all the way to the top floor.

Stepping off the elevator, it was clear we were all a little bit tipsy and having way too much fun to not get caught. We had to be echoing through the whole building, trying to sneak along the wall but not able to hold back giggles and talking. Someone gave up and snuck to the rail and started making "caw caw" noises at Cronin, and some guys even got bold and started yelling. "F-you, Crow!" echoed all over the atrium.

I've got to admit, it was hilarious to see his head pop up and look around, yelling, "Who's there?" into the dome of the hotel and trying to figure out how he missed us. I bet he jumped when we all got to our rooms and a half dozen hotel doors slammed at the same time.

That was the end of our first night hanging out with the Nickelback boys.

After "How You Remind Me" hit number one on the local rock station, we invited the whole band to come out and skate with us after practice at Nassau Coliseum. It was super fun to watch rock stars in their jeans skating around the ice, feeling like they were one of the boys. In return, they invited us over to a sound check across the street at Hofstra University. On the way over, Chad asked me if I wanted to sing with the band. My team was there, even my parents were there, and for just a minute, I got to be a rock star too.[20]

We had a game the next day, but we thought we could stay inconspicuous enough to watch just a few songs, even though they went on at eleven. I don't know whose brilliant idea it was to "borrow" straw cowboy hats from girls in the crowd—because that's the era when every girl had a straw cowboy hat—but that's what we did. Sure, all these six-foot-three guys across the street from the Nassau Coliseum were going to be less conspicuous in a crowd full of college kids and teens. Hats were *definitely* what we needed.

Undercover hats be damned, I don't know how many times I was still asked, "Don't you have a game tomorrow?"

It didn't matter anyway. The guys were waving and giving thumbs-up from the stage, and we were never going to be able to hide. It was the best of times—a couple of songs turned into the

---

20 I bet there's a video out there somewhere of me in a big red turtleneck sweater rocking out with Nickelback and singing their number-one hit. If you've got it, I'd love to see.

whole show, and then an invitation to hang out around the bus afterward. Then Chad pulled out mini motorcycles from under the tour bus that a handful of us tried to rip around on. Then more bands joined us, and it exploded into this full-on party in the parking lot, with shots and chugging and all kinds of fantastic madness. I remember having an in-depth conversation with Jerry Cantrell and the other guys from Alice in Chains. It was amazing.

Usually, I wouldn't even stay up late the night before a game, much less party. Exhausted and knowing I wouldn't be as rested as normal for the next day, I was mad at myself for breaking my routine and not continuing to prepare like a pro. But while I had been lying awake in bed anxious about breaking my routine, the rest of the team had apparently run into their own issues.

When our trainer walked into the room the next morning, he was hit with a wall of aftermath. One guy was rubbing antibacterial salve over his hands that had been scraped raw in a minibike tumble. A handful of guys had started arguing on the way home to their house that several of them shared, where apparently things got real. It turned into a big fight followed by a house meeting, all evidenced by black eyes and fat lips, and no sleep. The coaches had to know something was up. They never questioned us on it, though. They just let us have it.

My guilt was heavy, even without a coach's lecture. I fumbled through morning skate and tried to hide my exhaustion from the coaches. I tried to take a pre-game nap like usual, but I couldn't sleep. Something had to give. So as the game started, I made a deal with myself: *Don't get scored on, and shoot the puck every time it touches my stick. Don't get fancy—just get the*

puck, and rip it from everywhere on the ice. Hundred feet away?
Slapper. Go.

I think I wound up with seven shots on the net. We ended the game tied 2–2, but in the dressing room, you would have thought we had won something special.

I'm still friends with the Nickelback guys to this day. Chief and Ryan, the drummer, both came to my wedding. I've been in recording studios with them, gone on tour with them for a week pretending to be their security person, and got on stage shooting the t-shirt cannon. Years later, when I was living in Arizona, the band and crew came through for a tour stop in Phoenix, and we had them all out for steaks at the house. The entire tour—five buses of crew and band members at our house drinking wine and enjoying awesome homecooked food. Fellow hockey player Curtis Joseph stopped by with his kids, too, and we all had a blast the night before the show.

I think they cleaned out most of my wine collection that night. But they still showed up for the morning skate with the Coyotes and enjoyed meeting and sharing a few laughs with our coach, who happened to be Wayne Gretzky.

A few years after that, Chad declared an after-party at my house from the stage with some of the Coyotes and the band. At five in the morning, I had to kick Chad out so we could all sleep—I have a picture of him taking a box of Triscuit crackers and a whole container of jalapeño-spinach-artichoke dip[21] from my house while on the way to his plane to fly to the next show.

---

21 The good stuff from Costco. If you've had it, you know what I'm talking about. So good.

///

Around 2003, Garth Brooks came out with a foundation called Teammates for Kids. They reached out to our unions and asked players to donate money for every goal we scored or fight we got into. All of the money went right to the kids they were reaching with therapeutic and sports programs all over the country, so I donated something like a thousand dollars for every goal I scored as long as we were connected with his foundation. I stood behind the program and promoted them whenever I could. The whole team got on board, and Garth matched everything we donated from his pocket.

That era happened to be some of my best scoring, and a couple of years later, I wound up with more than twenty goals.

Halfway through that season, my parents were in town and out to lunch with my girlfriend, Brooke, and I when I got the call that Garth wanted us to come over to the Long Island Marriott. He had flown in on a private jet and rented out some space to say thank you to our entire team in person because that's just the type of guy Garth is. He's one of the most down-to-earth, humble guys I've ever met. He does incredible work for kids and charities around the world. You don't hear a lot about it, but you should because he's doing amazing things.

When we got there, it was just Garth and a couple of his people with about twenty-five chairs set up in a private suite. He had a guitar out and some beer, and he invited us to sit back and relax while he played some songs for about an hour.

At that time, Garth was at the height of his career, and we were sitting five feet away from him. We were sipping beer and relaxing while one of the greatest performers in the country played for us. He had just played for over a million people in Central Park in New York, but we were treated to a quiet, private show.

I stayed close to Teammates for Kids for a few years after that. Every year, he would treat us to something special as a way of saying thanks. Once, we stayed at the Venetian in Las Vegas, where all of the major sponsors and participating athletes got a private concert. Afterward, he would invite us up to play pool and hang out in his suite. He had the best stories about how he wrote his songs and things that happened behind the scenes.

Another time, he set up a dinner on stage at the Grand Ole Opry, just with ten or fifteen tables for players and sponsors. After dinner, the staff removed all of our dinner tables from the stage, and Garth and Trisha Yearwood played a private show for us in the Opry. It was just the hundred or so of us who had been there on the stage just a little bit before, enjoying dinner and getting to know each other. Afterward, we headed over to their home and barn to continue the celebration. I had a blast, and Tennessee-born Brooke soaked up every second.

Outside of any benefits for me, the charity itself was incredible and worth every dime. I was proud to be able to support it. But it was something special to see Garth match donations from his own pocket and with the huge sponsors he had on board and then thank us so thoughtfully and personally. I'm grateful to have been part of it all for so long.

///

Charity events continued to turn into interesting connections in my life. I wasn't ever as rich, famous, or wealthy as the other celebrities there, but I never really cared about that. I loved life and was just happy to be part of the experience.

The strangest and coolest encounter might have been the Washingtons—a mining family who were considered self-made billionaires. I met them back in '97 at a golf tournament, when Kevin and I hit it off and had a blast playing golf and hanging out. I don't get to hang out with Kevin and Kyle and their family often, but when I do, there's always a story. Just a couple of years ago, at Kyle's birthday party, there were fireworks, a guy riding jets into the sky, and women wearing mermaid tails swimming around the pool every morning during breakfast. I don't get surprised much anymore, but these guys are next level. And nothing will ever top the time Quincy Jones almost got us eaten by grizzly bears.

Around 2007, Kevin invited Brooke and me out to his family's private island less than a year after Olivia was born. They sent a plane to Vancouver, and it took us an hour up the coast to the island for a weekend away that was completely paid for. I had been to the island once before, but we had no idea what to expect that weekend.

As we landed in the float plane, we could see a full runway and a golf course, with a beautiful home perched on a cliff overlooking the inlet of the island. Pulling up to the dock, I saw actor Chris Tucker ripping around on a jet ski, screaming and having fun like Chris Tucker does. Pat Tillman's brother was roaming around the property. Quincy Jones was hanging out, and Herschel Walker was there with his wife and a couple of friends.

Someone on staff grabbed our bags for us and then told everyone else to get back on the plane. About a dozen of us gathered up with Mr. Washington, Kevin's dad, and flew out on a private float plane to meet a refurbished tugboat, the *St. Eval.* Mr. Washington explained that the boat had helped pull ships out of trouble during World War II.[22]

A bunch of dinghy boats were waiting to scoop us up and take us to the St. Eval, where a gorgeous breakfast was waiting for us. Everything was prepared down to the smallest detail, including the location of the boat. It was placed right in the middle of active sea life, where a pod of killer whales were breaching, diving, and playing like dolphins.

After an hour and a half of breakfast surrounded by orcas, it was time to move on to the next part of the trip. We made the trek back to the plane, which took us even farther north, toward Alaska. It landed in what looked to be completely untouched nature, where a small school bus was waiting to take us even deeper into the forest.

The bus pulled right up to a cage of fencing that extended over a stream below. The salmon were running just beneath our feet, and there were grizzly bears everywhere trying to catch them. They were so focused on their meal delivery that they didn't care about us. We got to stand there, just feet away,

---

22 Here's what one site says about it: "The former British tug *St. Eval*, now converted to a luxury yacht, sails into her home port of Vancouver. Originally built in Scotland in 1929, she had a long and colourful history as a tug in England. She was purchased in the early 1990s and converted in Seattle by Dennis Washington, owner of the Seaspan International marine empire based in Vancouver. She is 35m in length, 209 GT, and still flies the British flag." Shipspotting.com. 2007. "St. Eval – IMO 5070127." Published June 13, 2007. http://www.shipspotting.com/gallery/photo. php?lid=434037

smelling their fur and hearing the crunch as they snapped up fish out of the streams and ate them.

There were bears everywhere, but it felt completely safe. It was powerful and absolutely beautiful. The bus dropped us off at different viewing cages around the property, and we were totally captivated.

Before we went back to the island, the bus took us to a sand bar that stretched into the inlet. On either side, a stream ran at about four feet deep, and fifteen feet of stream away was another shoreline lined with grizzly bears. Our guide had a shotgun, and we had that distance of water, but there was nothing else to keep us safe.

The tour guides take that walk with new people every day and have done so for years. Ours explained how safe it was— just enough to keep you from panicking, but not enough to make you feel completely comfortable. After all, there was nothing but water between us and a shore full of massive predators. All sense of ease disappeared after ten minutes of enjoying this incredible experience when the tour guide looked down the sandbar and then said the two words you never want to hear from someone who's keeping you safe:

"Oh, shit."

A mama bear and her cubs had joined us on the sandbar back where the bus had let us off. She wasn't paying any attention to us yet, but she *was* blocking our only way back to the bus. We had to get around her or we couldn't get home.

We were terrified. If the guide was, he didn't show us. He told us if we stayed together, it would look like we were one big bear, and she would leave us alone.

For a few minutes of slowly walking toward the mama and her cubs, huddled together, we thought we were okay. Brooke was terrified—by that point, we were married and had a little baby waiting for us at home. As much as the mama bear would protect her cubs, my mama bear wanted to get back to hers. It was our first time away from Olivia, and there was a definite sense that this could go terribly wrong.

Quincy wasn't having it, either.

When the grizzly stood up on her hind legs—just like you see in the movies, clearly getting a whiff of our scent—we lost all sense of calm. Quincy took off, with his bad hips, determined to hobble to safety faster than we were moving, mumbling, "Bears don't like Black people," the whole way. It might have been funny if it didn't feel so real. Instead, Brooke was crying, and our guide was yelling at Quincy to stop and then screaming into the walkie for backup while Quincy kept trying to run away.

Some ATVs came flying around the corner of the inlet toward the sandbar, and more guides fired shotguns into the air to try to distract the mama bear. All that did was scare the cubs, but it was enough to get them running away from where we needed to be. Mama bear was just there to keep them in line and get them fed, so she followed, and we were able to get back to safety. I've never been so happy to see a short yellow bus in my life.

Back safe and sound, the rest of the weekend was so relaxing. I listened in awe as Quincy talked about his journey through the music world and what it was like producing the *Thriller* album with Michael Jackson. I empathized as we heard how Pat Tillman must have been killed by friendly fire—and come to find out, he was. I pinched myself as the best meals

I've ever had just kept coming out to us, created and made by chefs who lived full time on the island. I watched Herschel live out his daily routine since he still played in the NFL. He had learned at a young age that eating less gave him more energy, so he started eating like a lion—one meal to sustain him for a whole day. He trained like one, too, even on a mini vacation.[23]

Coming from where I did as a kid, that kind of adventure and extravagance and dedication could have been a shock—but it always felt like an easy fit. The celebrities were all just people like me, and I was lucky to get to experience some seriously amazing things with them. They inspired me to want to do more, be more, and create more impact in my life and the lives of others so I could treat my family and friends to adventures like these one day.

///

For every adventure I've gone on, having Brooke by my side made it that much better. She came into my life at just the right time, and we were inseparable from the beginning. Back when a mutual friend of ours first wanted to introduce us, I asked, "Is she marriage material? I don't want to meet any other girls if they're not marriage material."

She absolutely was.

---

23 Herschel meant business, on the field and off. He would do up to 3,500 push-ups and sit-ups a day, and I can vouch for his dedication. NFL. "Football Fit: A look at Herschel Walker's workout routine." Published September 23, 2015. http://www.nfl.com/news/story/0ap3000000537126/article/football-fit-a-look-at-herschel-walkers-workout-routine

If we had met each other a decade earlier, when she was traveling the world as a model and I was trying to make the NHL, who knows if we would have connected. With her family in the eastern US and mine on the west coast of Canada, maybe we wouldn't have met at all. Out of all of the thousands of interesting people we've both met over the years, in all of the amazing places we've been, our paths crossed at exactly the right time and place.

At first, we spent a few months talking on the phone and hanging out with groups of models or teammates around us, but we were never able to find time for a real date. So when the all-star break came around that year and none of my buddies were available to return to South Beach with me, I took a leap of faith.

Brooke had just gotten back from working for Oscar de la Renta, and she said she was totally up for a trip. We had barely been alone together and had never even kissed. But we said goodnight to each other every night and talked every day that we could. We knew each other well, and lounging by the pool in South Beach, it showed. There, we told each other everything about our lives, our parents, our beliefs, and our dreams that hadn't already spilled out in months of phone conversations.

I couldn't believe how much our values aligned. As different as we were as people, our core values matched up perfectly. I actually snuck away to call my sister and tell her I had met my future wife. She just laughed and asked me how much I'd had to drink.[24] But at the same time, Brooke was calling her parents to tell them she'd met her soulmate.

---

24 Okay, I was a few drinks in. It was Miami.

Teasing turned to more serious conversations about what kind of wedding she wanted and how we could do this the right way.

I remember telling her, "I already know I'm going to marry you, so let's just do it."

She didn't disagree. It was inevitable. If a wedding hadn't been so important to her, we might have run off to Las Vegas right then.

It took two or three more years for that timing to be right, and once again, it was more than worth the wait. We'd go to fashion week in Paris together in the off-season, and she'd travel with me when she could too. We had a ton of fun just dating and enjoying time together, knowing that we were always going to be together no matter when the wedding made it official.

Since she wanted something simple for the wedding, I decided to go all out for the proposal. I pictured us taking a helicopter ride to the top of a glacier in Whistler, BC, where I'd get down on one knee and give her the gorgeous ring I'd designed for her. But the weather was too bad for my plans to work, and in our two-bedroom penthouse, I was sure she was going to find the ring before it cleared up enough to fly.

So when her mom came up to visit, knowing how close they were, I decided it was time. Like, *right* then. At the last second, when we were all heading out for dinner together.

I called one of my best friends from my hometown, who was now a successful stunt man in Vancouver. I said, "Todd, I need a big favor."

Petals leading from the door to the fireplace...candles all over the apartment and on the wraparound deck...lights definitely dimmed...a Sarah McLaughlin song cued up...Make it a fairytale, but don't burn my house down.

"Can you do that?"

He told me yeah, and Brooke, her mom, and I got ready for a dinner that would kill enough time for him to work. But as we pulled out of the parking garage, I could see Todd's truck pulling in behind me—and the silhouette of whatever girl he was dating at the time.

We went to a lounge that made all these cool, crazy drinks, and under any other circumstances, it would have been great. But I had to give him a few hours to get everything done, and every time I texted him to check in, Brooke wanted to know who I was texting and why I wouldn't tell her.

The thing you have to know about Todd is that he had a reputation with the ladies. He was a stunt man and a super cool dude who always had someone new on his arm. So when I arrived back at the apartment just a few minutes too early, I could see Todd and a girl ducking down in the apartment. When we saw Todd's truck, a full "He'd better not have some girl up there!" rant ensued. Brooke wanted to know everything, and I had to play dumb while I circled around the block another time to give him a chance to leave.

The truck was gone when we got back, and Brooke was completely confused now. I tried to get us up the elevator as quickly as I could without answering any questions directly, while signaling to her mom to get her camera ready. Since she had no idea what I was planning and had a couple of cocktails in her, too, she just looked at me like I had five heads.

When she saw all of the candles and roses, Brooke's first reaction was confusion at having seen Todd's truck. There weren't tears or romantic thoughts. Nope. She was just massively confused.

"What's going on in here? Was there a party? Are we having a party? *What did Todd do?* What is this?"

Instead of telling her what I was thinking—*No, babe, this is the greatest proposal ever!*—I told her to just follow the petals. Fortunately, Todd had delivered so much better than I thought he would on such short notice.

We made it down the hallway and into a room overlooking the whole city. The fireplace was going, and our song was playing. The ring box was perched on a beautiful wine decanter filled with miniature marshmallows. It looked like it was on a bed of clouds, popped open and sparkling.

Her mom caught on before Brooke did, and she stayed in the hallway snapping pictures and giving us space to have our moment in private. It was a magical night. Brooke called her dad to tell him she was getting married and that she was so happy. We both were.

Our wedding was on the beach in Cabo San Lucas, with our friends and family watching, near the house that I had bought down there. Oscar de la Renta made Brooke's wedding dress for her, and more than eighty people flew to Cabo to enjoy the celebration: friends and family, teammates, and people we loved. Everything was gorgeous—her, the wedding, this life we were going to build together. It was one of the best weeks of my life, and I couldn't have stepped into the next phases of my life without her by my side.

CHAPTER EIGHT

FROM THE PENTHOUSE TO THE OUTHOUSE

I played the best hockey of my life on the Island. By the end of 2003, I led my team with twenty-seven goals and was on top of the world. And the very next year, I was kicked back to the fourth line.

That season, a new coach came on board—Peter Laviolette—who had other things in mind for us. When he first took over the team, he traded people, moved people up, and sent people back, myself included. He sat me down in his office and threw out some obscure player's name. He told me, "That's the kind of player you could be in this league. The guy who draws penalties and takes guys down."

I should have told him, "I have twenty-seven goals. You've got the wrong guy." As hard as it is to admit, I just took it. I didn't stand up for myself like I should have. I didn't demand more ice time. I kept my previous mindset that I was lucky to be there—that team should be first and you don't rock the boat—and that mentality hurt my career. Now that I know how short an NHL career can be, I wish I had demanded the ice time I deserved. I should have continued to play with first- and second-line players as opposed to being relegated to playing on the third or fourth line with less-skilled players. Everything I did was for the team—to fight, score, and play my ass off so we could shift the dynamics back to the winning ways of that dynasty from the eighties.

A year and just thirteen goals later, I was a free agent looking for a new home. I signed with Boston in 2005, and Brooke let her modeling career go so she could come with me. We bought a brownstone downtown, just across from Tom Brady's place, and made plans to settle in.

I could have signed with the Rangers for more money, Toronto for a five-year deal, or Nashville to be near Brooke's family, but I chose Boston. In retrospect, the Rangers were probably the better fit. They made all kinds of promises about making me an assistant captain and putting me on the second line. But the Rangers hadn't made the playoffs in eight years, while Boston had just re-signed Joe Thornton, Glen Murray, and Andrew Raycroft. The team looked great. If it meant playing on the third line there for a few years, then that was a chance at the Cup that I didn't want to pass up. At least that's what my thought process was.

That's what decided it for me. Not the money. Not the length of the contract. Nothing mattered except the possibility that we could win a Stanley Cup.

But it wasn't to be. Sixteen games into the season, I got a call in the middle of the night telling me I'd been traded to Wayne Gretzky's team in Phoenix. I had to be on a flight the next morning to meet the team in San Jose for a game.

This is probably my biggest regret in my career: that I didn't know how to stand up for myself as a player. Sure, I played through injuries and hid my pain. But outside of that, I kept my mouth shut for the good of the team. I was taught that hard work and selflessness were all that mattered. It wasn't in my DNA to just look out for number one. It was always a little bit shocking to me when teams didn't return the respect I had for them. It was a little bit shocking when the team didn't repay me for doing something for "the right reasons" and not for the money or the personal gain.

What I didn't realize yet was just how short a hopeful ten-year career could be. When you're in the NHL, you take every moment for everything you can get. You can never just be a cog in the wheel that doesn't disrupt anything. That just makes you unseen. It makes you look like a fourth-line player who doesn't want to rock the boat—so that's exactly where they put you. They treated me like a piece of meat. I was expendable.

My wife was brushing her teeth for bedtime when we got the phone call and I told her what was happening. It was ten thirty, and they said I was playing in San Jose with the Coyotes the next night at seven.

I was furious. They knew I could've signed anywhere. They knew I was there to help them win a Cup. More importantly, I knew I could've made a better choice. Any of those other teams really wanted me, and Boston had been the least excited about it. They did win the Stanley Cup a few years later, so my instincts were right. But that shouldn't have been my only consideration.

Even with my wife crying and me upset as well, I had to spend all night packing. She would catch up to me later, with the brownstone rented out and everything she knew left behind.

A stick boy met me at Boston Gardens that night to load up my equipment, though they didn't leave me with a jersey and even withheld a few of my sticks to save money. I got home around midnight and had a five o'clock car service to the airport. On next to no sleep, with flights all day, my anger turned to nerves and excitement as I worked up the energy for my first game with the Coyotes.

The pre-game meal in the hotel was just starting when I got there, and my childhood idol invited me to sit at his table. Gretz told me how happy he was to have traded for me, and we talked all through lunch. Tyson Nash was there, as well as Shane Doan and a couple of other guys I knew. They welcomed me to the team, and I was excited to show them what I could do. I managed a half-hour nap after lunch, and then it was time to go.

///

Out of the six hundred-plus games that I played in my career, few of them started with me feeling 100 percent. That's just how it goes. Something's bruised or broken or battered, or you flew the night before or were sick. I saw guys play through broken bones, knocked-out teeth, broken noses. You just play.

In fact, when I was really tired or hurt, my game was actually better. I had to stay focused on a simple game so I could get into another gear.

I wanted to make a good first impression with Wayne and the team, but my emotions were wrecked. I wound up hitting and cross-checking one of the Sharks players and then getting jumped by Scott Thornton, a tough kid who was playing for the Sharks. He got the jump on me and got the best of me in the fight, but I scored a nice goal later on in the game and definitely showed my team that I was willing to battle for them.

That game wound up being one of the few highlights of my time in Phoenix.

Another—one I had dreamed about since I was a kid and will remember until the day I die—was when Gretz came out for a practice in his real gear rather than his usual tracksuit and loosely tied skates. There he was, the Wayne Gretzky of my childhood, with his iconic "paddle" stick and his eyes on me. "Scatch," he said, "you're my centerman today. You'd better be on your game!"

For the most part, he'd kept me on the fourth line in games, and I didn't have a lot of time to settle in and show off what I could do. But for that practice, I got to play center for my coach and lifelong idol, who still played perfectly even though it had been years since he had been on a team. I threw him hard passes and watched him handle them like a dream. Over and over again, he threw perfect passes for me to one-time into the goal—probably fifteen or twenty goals in that one practice. For that hour and a half, I lived out my childhood dream. Maybe not exactly the way I'd imagined it, but just as special as I could've asked.

Gretz was an amazing human and the greatest player in the world, but we didn't connect well as a coach and player. He didn't really know how to use me, and I never figured out how to advocate for myself. It wasn't my best hockey or team chemistry. I wish he could have seen me play my best hockey. I was actually a shooter, and it seemed like wingers he would pair me up with were shooters as well, so when I gave them the puck, most of the time it wasn't coming back to me, which wasn't as conducive to me scoring goals. I could never really find the same type of chemistry with any line mates on the Coyotes like I had found with Jason Blake and Jason Weimer from my Islander days.

The worst of it came when I got hit face-first into the glass for what would become my fourth concussion, a little more than halfway through my second season with the Coyotes. Immediately, fluid started to pour out of my nose—not blood or mucus, but something orange and sticky. Trainers and doctors were concerned that it might be a cerebrospinal fluid leak. They were all really concerned, and they couldn't see a way to take care of it.[25]

For a year and a half after that, I couldn't find my balance. I actually did speak up to the trainers and the team about how something was off in my spine. I felt drunk all the time. We did MRIs and all kinds of tests to see if my neck or skull had

---

25 To this day, I still get a little bit of a leak out of my nose if I move in a certain way. We're working on testing and fixing it still.

fractured, but they couldn't see why I was getting this leaking or how my neck and spine were out of alignment. No one knew what to do.

I thought it would eventually go away, so when Phoenix called me to ask how I was, I reflexively told them, "I'm great! Ready to go." What else could I say? There were no other tests to run or treatments to do. I had to work it out. It had to just go away.

Ten minutes later, they sent my agent notice that they were buying out the rest of my contract. My claim to be healthy meant they had permission to buy me out, where honesty about still being injured would have kept me on the roster and not allowed them to buy me out. Even my agent suggested filing a grievance—he knew I wasn't ready to go. But when we talked about our options, we thought I could just get another two-year deal at the league minimum and move on at the same time. After all, I was lifting weights and trying to gain some strength back. I wasn't feeling bad. I just couldn't get my balance quite right.

What I didn't know—and really it's still just secondhand information—was that Gretzky and Maloney were telling teams I'd never play again.

Maybe they wanted the best for me. Maybe they just couldn't vouch for me in good faith, though that would be an interesting justification after they cut me on the pretense of health. Whatever their reasoning, I was totally surprised. I still felt like I could play—I just had to figure out how to get my body back to working normally again.

"I'm fine. Let's go" had been my mantra for so long. I wasn't sure what could be on the other side if I *wasn't* actually fine.

///

After that fourth concussion pulled me out of Phoenix, I tried to skate with the Rangers. But something still wasn't right, and they never brought me out of the minors.

Financially, thanks to all those real estate investments over the years, we were okay. We had the house in Boston fully rented, two houses in Vancouver rented to movie stars, and a house in Cabo renting for big money too. Plus, the contract buyout from the Coyotes kept some money coming in, just not as much as if I were still active with them. Cash flow was not a problem. So did I really want to fight my body to keep playing?

Brooke and I went back to Vancouver for a couple of months and explored the idea of retiring. Maybe Gretz was right. Maybe I was done. Or maybe I just needed a break to let my spine and neck and jaw heal again.

I even had something to do while I waited. Eric Lindros called me from the NHL Players Association. He'd heard I was done playing and asked if I would like to work with the union as a divisional player rep. I would be the go-between for six teams and the union. In other words, I could still be part of the game in some way, and my mind would have something to stay busy with. It sounded like a great transition.

I really loved my time working with the players and serving them, but there were a lot of politics and bureaucracy going on that made the job not fun at all. But in the process, I connected with Geoff Courtnall, who had concussion problems. He told me about a German doctor in Seattle, named Dietrich Klinghardt. "I think I know a guy who can help your head. I've been to eighteen doctors for my concussions, and he knows what he's doing. Just...stay open-minded."

Open-minded?

"Oh, and he looks like the guy from *Back to the Future* with the big white hair, and one of the treatments is called the Crown of Thorns."

Got it.

The price—twenty grand for a weekend—and the quirks couldn't stop me. They were nothing compared to being stuck in this unbalanced body that couldn't work out anymore, couldn't even jog, and definitely couldn't play.

In June, I flew to Seattle, and Dr. Klinghardt told me, "I can fix that."

He pointed to my C5 and said words like *occiput* and explained things about my spine and jaw that I still barely understand. What I heard most was that word *fix* and his reassurances. Then he got to work.

For hours at a time, he would run megadose IV bags through my veins. He'd have me lie on magnetic blankets. He'd do spinal and jaw manipulation, like a chiropractic adjustment. For about five days, we alternated and repeated all kinds of treatments. We did megadosing of vitamins, a mouth guard, and a dental split for TMJ that seemed to help balance my upper cervical spine by bracing my jaw. Then at the end of it all, he sent me to a guy who could work on my head.

Imagine someone shoving popsicle sticks with balloons attached to them up my nostrils—I don't know what exactly he did, but that's what it looked like. Then the popsicle sticks came out, and the balloons were left hanging from my nostrils, and he attached the ends to something like the pump for a blood pressure cuff.

Whatever the terminology is, the pressure inside my nasal cavity grew and grew until the plates in my face felt like they popped out—like twelve broken noses and four concussions had dented my face in, and now the front of it was all back in place. Then he sent me back over to Dietrich for one more treatment, which they said would get me back on track. It was called the Crown of Thorns.

The Crown of Thorns, thankfully, is not named for a device, but for how you look during the procedure. Dietrich took a syringe and an extra-long needle and started to inject a substance in increments all around my head. In each place where the needle punctured my skin, little trickles of blood ran down my face, like a crown of thorns had just been removed.

The last injection went into my temples, and when I say it went in, I mean I'm not sure exactly where a six-inch needle could possibly go as it disappeared into my temples. But it went somewhere as I held my jaw open at a particular angle. It felt like he was spraying something onto my brain—if that's even a sensation you can identify.

When I sat up, he did one more alignment adjustment on my jaw, and the difference was immediate. I walked out of his office and just...kept walking. Then jogging. Then running. I ran five miles straight, feeling every ray of sun and every pump of my legs. *This is how I used to feel!* It all came flooding back like nothing had happened, followed quickly by the most exciting thought I'd had in months:

What if I could make a comeback?

///

I thought about it over the summer, as my body and balance continued to come back to me. Then, with a month to go before training camp, I scrounged together whatever leftover hockey equipment I could find and took it to some drop-in ice time at a community center. Stick and puck time. They didn't expect anyone to have equipment, and anyone with seven bucks could play around on the rink.

I was too afraid of hurting myself to go without equipment, though, so in my full equipment, I skated around teenagers in jogging pants, holding the puck that I'd purchased at the front desk on the way in. Then I dropped it on the ice, batted it around for a second, and pulled back to take my first shot in a year and a half.

That thing *sailed*.

It was like a laser beam flying from one end of the rink to the other. It flew in the air the whole length of the rink, from the bottom of the face-off circle on one end to the other, and then hit perfectly between the crossbar and the post. It was a perfectly placed shot like every young hockey player dreams of, except from two hundred feet away. It was crazy for anyone, especially after a year and a half off.

I couldn't do it again in a million years.

I looked up toward the sky and thought, *All right, God. Are we doing this?*

My attention came back down to earth when a little kid who was about eight years old skated up to me and said, "Whoa, you're really good."

I took a deep breath and smiled. "I haven't played in a little while. Want to help me practice?"

Off we went, passing the puck back and forth to each other, shooting it into the net, cheering each other on. He was amazed at how hard I could shoot the puck, so I told him about the teams I'd been on and how long I'd played. He was amazed, and he was a fun little guy to come back with. He asked me questions, and I gave him pointers on technique and some skills as we skated around together. When it was time to be done, I handed him my Dave Scatchard patterned stick and left.

As soon as I got home, I told my wife what had happened. I told her what I knew to be true the second I stepped out of that doctor's office. I had to try to make a comeback.

Dave Scatchard

TACO BELL.

Portland Winterhawks - 95-96   Tr He...   19

*Wearing C as the team captain for the Portland Winterhawks
just a couple of years after barely making the team.*

The emotional home opener and first Islanders game after 9/11.

Mariusz Czerkawski, Brooke, and me with actor Kevin "Chappy" Chapman out for one of our many amazing New York dinners. "Chow" was one of my favorite teammates, a great player, and he really taught me how to really enjoy the finer things in life.

Me running a sound check with Nickelback after they practiced on the ice with us that morning.

Brooke and me hanging with Garth Brooks in his Las Vegas suite during his Teammates for Kids charity event.

The newest Boston Bruin. Loved the city; love the people— unfortunately my stay was much too short.

Our wedding day, June 15, 2005, in Cabo San Lucas, Mexico. I'll never forget the love and support we felt from friends and teammates. Brooke was wearing a dress that Oscar De La Renta had made for her.

CHAPTER NINE

THE COMEBACK KID

Without an agent, I didn't know where to start. I called my former teammate and former Islanders goalie Garth Snow, who was now their GM. He had seen me lead the team in goals, but he didn't do anything to try to help me. He flatly told me that there wasn't enough room to make space for me at camp. It was a lie that changed my view of him as an ex-teammate, but there was nothing I could do.

Next, I called the Canucks directly and explained my situation to Mike Gillis. I explained my health and that I wanted to come play for him. While he couldn't give me anything concrete, he did offer me a free-agent tryout.

Without an agent or a contract or anything but gratitude, I walked on to start skating with that generation of Canucks.

I fell right back into workouts like I hadn't missed a beat. I used the last two weeks before training camp to get acclimated with the guys and try to get back up to speed with the fast NHL pace. Guys like Darcy Hordichuk, Kevin Bieksa, and Alexander Burrows made me feel right at home. They helped me fit right in as training camp began, and after a few quick practices, we jumped right into exhibition games. I had a great early exhibition game against San Jose, scoring a goal on my first shift. I even jumped in to fight Jody Shelly when he was about to kill Alex Burrows.[26]

After a couple of those kinds of outings, I was playing well enough to make the team. But my body was having difficulty with the torque I was putting on it. I had been unable to train up until just a few weeks before then.

The Canucks had me slotted to play another game, but my groin muscles were so tight that I was concerned about them tearing and taking me out for months. Skating my heart out every day pushed my muscles beyond their abilities. Instead of pushing through like I had before, I told the trainer about it.

"Just give me one day to recover, and then I'll be able to finish camp."

Next thing I knew, I was in the office being told "thanks but no thanks" due to my health history. They informed me they were going to release me, and that I had given them an easy

---

26 The bad thing was, that got me kicked out of that game for third man in, and I didn't get to finish the game, only playing a few shifts before getting sent to the showers.

out. If I had been able to play a great game that night, it would have been harder. Yet another bad breakup. "Anyone would be lucky to have you....it was a tough decision...you're going to be fine...it's just not a good fit for us right now..."

I had a home there. I loved the team. I was playing well. It would have been a perfect scenario. I went home and cried.

Their words weren't empty, though. I had played well enough that they were sure I was going to get a spot right away without dipping into the minors, otherwise they would have given me a two-way contract. Mike Gillis did the stand-up thing and offered to spread the word that I was healthy again. That didn't get me a one-way that would keep me in the NHL, but it did mean a lot to me. I will always be grateful for that.

When Nashville called offering me a two-way contract and an opportunity to play a lot, I took it. I wasn't as enthusiastic about *playing till I die* in the minors anymore, but it was something. And that something was what I had been looking for since that last concussion knocked me down for so long. I just needed to play.

///

My time in the minors took us to Milwaukee, and the move from Phoenix wasn't the only adjustment I had to make. Last time I was in the minors, I was the younger one. Now I was thirty-four years old, checking my stock portfolio and managing rental houses while the young kids were talking about the video games that just came out. They were great kids, but they were absolutely kids. They were part of a different generation entirely, and I could see it in the way they trained and played.

Then there was the way Nashville ran its two-way. I actually spent a decent amount of time playing in Nashville, even though I wasn't on a one-way deal. Playing was actually a blast, especially once I paired up with Cal O'Reilly, a really skilled player who loved to pass the puck and was really smart on the ice. He was good enough to be in the NHL but just couldn't find a long-term home. When we found a rhythm, I felt like I was going to score in every single game—twenty goals and ten assists in thirty-six games in the minors, and three goals and two assists in my sixteen games in the NHL. More than enough to play in the league.

But if you stayed up with an NHL team for thirty days straight, the team was supposed to pay your rent or mortgage. So I'd get called up and would play really well for twenty-seven, twenty-eight, twenty-nine days...then they'd send me back for the weekend. It saved them money to shift me back and forth versus having me there on the NHL-level salary, and they'd save the commitment of having me there long term. There was always another third- or fourth-line guy they could bring up in my place so my time could reset.

And every time they'd send me down to Nashville, I had to leave my wife and now three little kids by themselves up in Wisconsin. Olivia was four. Caden was turning two, and Sawyer was just turning one. I'd come home for a little while and then kiss them goodbye and take off again without really knowing how long it would be. For weeks at a time, they would be stuck in the ice and snow alone in a two-bedroom apartment.

It's smart business, I guess, but it's not a great way to cultivate a player's best hockey—or a team's, for that matter.

///

I had spent years playing through injuries and hiding what was really going on in my body. The league taught me well. Honesty could jeopardize your career, so I went back to keeping pain to myself as much as I could. When the puck drops, you can do almost anything.

In 2009, I played well in a game for the Admirals against the Abbotsford Heat. I scored late in the game to close the gap, but then in the last shift, one of my teammates accidentally ran into me. His helmet broke three of my ribs. Because they told me I was going to get called up to Nashville for the next game, I kept my mouth shut about the injury.

I just needed to get through the next game. With practice in between. Which included conditioning.

I arrived in Nashville wanting to make a good impression, and on the first day of practice, there was an emphasis on conditioning. The guys were going pretty hard at their off-ice conditioning, all supervised by the strength coach and one of the assistant coaches.

Every rep felt like a knife into my lungs. After ripping off twelve or fifteen wide-grip pull-ups, I made sure the guys couldn't see the tears in my eyes. And I kept going. I didn't want to be the guy who quits when it gets hard. I kept going until I had played the whole call-up with broken ribs. Three weeks later, near that one-month mark when I knew they'd send me down, I finally went to the trainer for x-rays. The x-ray tech confirmed the broken ribs and was surprised I hadn't come in earlier to have them checked. Then she told me that the worst was over. I just kept playing through it, not mentioning it to anybody again.

I've played with broken bones in my feet, a broken nose, broken cheekbones. I've played with a cast on my arm when I broke a thumb in the middle of the tryouts for Team Canada.[27] I've had well over a hundred stitches in my face, multiple concussions, and twelve broken noses. I've broken an orbital bone in my face, knocked out four teeth, dislocated my jaw, and broke my collarbone. My biceps tendon has torn and reattached, multiple torn labrums and broken ribs, surgery on my shoulders with re-separation, a broken sternum, hollow heels and a bone graft, broken feet from slap shots, broken forearm and thumb, and detached tendon on my thumb, plus MCL tears in both knees and pulled and strained groins.

For the biggest part of my career, any one of those injuries would happen, and I'd just keep playing. But the more my head was messed with, the less my body could take. After the fourth concussion, something about my balance and alignment stayed off—even after the Crown of Thorns treatment, my body wasn't quite right. The night that Carlo sucker-punched me made that clear.

Carlo Colaiacovo wasn't a tough guy, but he was big and strong and suited for defense. One night with Nashville, after

---

27 I got close on Team Canada a couple of times, but none so bad as the time that I was sure the opportunity had passed and decided to go ahead with Lasik eye surgery. Sure enough, lying in bed recovering, Steve Tambolini called me up to congratulate me, and I couldn't take it. Who knows where my career would have gone if I'd been able to go. I'm sure there was a reason it didn't work out, and I wouldn't trade my career for the world.

out-muscling Carlo to get to the front of the net and scoring a goal, I was in the middle of celebrating my goal during one of my call-ups when he came up and suckered me in the face so hard I broke my nose again. I dropped my gloves from pure reflex and started giving it back to him while he turtled on the ice to cover up. I was so pissed off—he was one of the last guys I thought would jump me, especially after I scored. I have no idea what he was thinking.

Realistically, he had likely given me another concussion, though I never had it diagnosed or labeled at all. It gave me whiplash for sure, and I had pounding headaches for days.

Flying out to Columbus the next night, I was mentally foggy enough that it felt like I was floating. Something was off in my head, but if I told anyone, I was sure they'd send me down. So I played. The game was fine as long as I tried not to run into anyone or touch them. The entire game seemed like a blur to me, like I was there but I wasn't there. It was an eerie feeling.

I tried to keep it simple and make the easy play, and that turned into a solid game. I thought I was in the clear and wouldn't be found out while my head got back to normal, but something caught me off guard. Actually, *someone* caught me. On the plane ride home, one of our skills guys, Steve Sullivan, started a poker game. I am always one to buy into a poker game and have even played in many World Series of Poker tournaments. So when I didn't want to play, it was a big red flag for him. I told him I wasn't feeling well, and he immediately asked if it was from the sucker punch the night before.

I had such a bad migraine the next day that I couldn't practice, but I told the trainers that I had whiplash and couldn't turn my head. I was just hoping for another day to recover. The next day, they sent me back down to the minors.

If you're not a professional athlete, it's easy enough to step back when you're injured and be honest about what's going on. If I'm playing with buddies today, I'll tell them if I'm not 100 percent, and I'll take breaks to heal. But you can't do that when it's your job. They're going to bring someone else in, or they're going to cut you because you're always hurt. So I did exactly what I was supposed to. I played through pain. I played even though my brain clearly needed a break. I did everything I could for them, and the second they got a whiff of an excuse, they'd send me back. Over and over. Up and down all year long just so they could save some money. I was just a pawn to them.

I finished that up-and-down season playing as good as I could possibly play. I scored twenty goals in the minors and three goals in my sixteen games in the NHL, which was on pace for fifteen or more if they had kept me. I felt like I deserved a one-way contract. When it came time to re-sign, that's exactly what I told them. And they refused.

There were a lot of times with various organizations that I felt like the teams were just using me for their own benefit—not as someone who was valued in the organization. Not as part of a team. Nashville had seemed like such a good fit, but it wasn't meant to be.

In their eyes, it was too risky for them to pay someone like that. To pay me. "You're at that age now where your body's just going to break down," they explained.

I didn't buy it. I called around for a one-way contract with another team. My agent called around. Lots of teams had been asking about me, and I was sure we could turn that into the type of deal I wanted. The closest thing I could get was an offer from St. Louis. They had more money in their minors and something of a guarantee. Plus I still had the chance to make the Blues in a training camp.

As soon as I signed and got started, it was clear that they just wanted to use me to mentor their young guys in the minors. I could tell in training camp when they started playing me with their fourth-line guys that they were not serious about giving me a chance to make the team out of training camp. I only got called up to St. Louis a few times, and even in the minors, Jared Bednar was not playing me very much. It was the exact opposite of having Layne Lambert as the head coach in Milwaukee the year before, who always asked for my input and valued it and gave me ice time.

That year in Peoria was the worst year of hockey I ever had.

I hadn't been told the truth about the opportunity that they were going to give me. They weren't planning on keeping me up at all, unless there was some natural disaster that got in their way. I played with fourth-line guys and rookies all training camp, never really getting an opportunity to succeed.

On one of the call-ups to St. Louis, Jamal Mayers, who was playing with the Blackhawks at the time, took out my right knee and gave me a third-degree tear in my MCL It seemed to take forever, and I did almost all my rehab back in Peoria. I don't think I got called up again after that for the rest of the year.

That's when, with just four games to go in the season, still playing in Peoria, I sustained my worst and last hockey injury ever. My fifth concussion, which knocked me unconscious, ended my career, and ended my life as I knew it.

I remember the puck dropping at center ice. I remember skating forward as fast as I could, stickhandling the puck and moving it onto my backhand. But then that's it. The next thing I remember is being in a black void with the sensation of floating up, looking down on my crumpled body on the ice as the paramedics and my trainer worked on me.

I watched them wheel me off.

I hadn't seen the hit coming and didn't have time to process what was happening, but I felt my life slip away from me as my body left the arena. In one blow, I'd lost everything—including my life.

On the other side of the void was something I'll never be able to explain fully. I've tried. After years of silence, not even sure where to begin, I finally started to share bits and pieces of what I experienced. First with Mattias and his wife, and then with Brooke. Eventually, I began working on this book, opened up to clients, and touched on it at speaking events. I've even spoken to some other people who died and came back. Each time, I get some more words and ways to describe what I saw and felt. Each time, there is so much left unsaid—so much that you just can't know without being there.

We've all heard the "go toward the light" stories, but what they don't tell you is that the light is more than what we understand light to be. It wasn't a metaphorical movement or the appearance of light. It was more real than anything I've ever felt on earth but so surreal that there's nothing to compare it to.

There was a definite sensation of leaving my body. I was moving somewhere—like traveling upward through a tunnel in complete darkness. When the tunnel opened up, I was both consumed and surrounded by a light so pure and expansive that it felt alive. It was shining directly into me and exploding out of me, but all around me too. Without fully seeing a physical form, it was clearly a presence of God. While clearly feeling physical sensations as I'd never experienced them before, it felt like being held.

For what seemed like forever and also just a moment, I was curled up like a child in my parents' arms. I almost didn't feel like I deserved to be there, but I felt my hair being stroked and heard a soothing, "It's going to be okay. Everything's going to be okay." As I relaxed into the arms that held me, it was the most belonging, welcoming, and inclusive reception I had ever received. I knew that I was coming home.

I was in the presence of love, creation, wholeness, and peace. There was no need for time; it just was...expansiveness, openness, oneness, and being connected to all things with shining light on everything. Words weren't needed.

The light surrounded me, filled me, and became part of me. It overflowed from my body and exploded into the space around me—a space that had no form but was expansive, stretching and reaching out into everything. The rules were different there. There *were* no rules. Every limit I'd ever experienced was gone. Everything was wide open, with no boundaries, no beginnings or endings. Walls, forms, words, weight—in place of all of those limitations was just...love.

The light was love. The presence was unconditional compassion. I curled up into those arms and let that love take my breath away, while at the same time breathing more freely than I ever had in my life.

It was pure ecstasy and bliss and joy and peace and beauty... and I cried.

I laughed and I cried and I breathed. I had no idea why it was all happening to me, and I also knew it was exactly how life was meant to be from the very beginning. How it was supposed to happen to all of us. How it was the only pure thing a soul could experience—the way things were before the pain and anger and hurt could weigh us down.

I had lived an incredible life in my thirty-some years, but *this*...this was beyond any of it. A state of completion and being that I didn't know was possible.

The most complete, incredible moments in life show us glimpses of that side of existence. When my first child was born. When my second child caught his first fish. When my third child was conceived. When I was just a little kid and knew that someone was talking to me, always there for me—at least until my dad told me I was too old for that kind of imaginary thing.

I remember telling "my friend" goodbye and never hearing those voices again. I remember the reality of parenting hitting and life getting difficult. For every miraculous moment, there seems to be a hundred difficult ones, and most of us only get flickers of the beauty that we're meant to experience.

This was different. It was a place I could stay. I could finally get some rest.

I cried, and I laughed. I felt free, and I felt guilty. I suddenly realized that nothing I'd ever done had actually mattered. I'd focused on the wrong things for most of my life—and the love didn't care. God didn't care. The light didn't dim, and no one abandoned me just because I felt unworthy. I knew I'd had it wrong all along, and so did he, and he was still proud of me anyway.

The freedom and weightlessness of that moment picked up everything that I'd ever carried on my shoulders, in my heart, and within my body and carried it away. I felt the light pour through the spaces that were left in me and clean up every hurt, every memory, every regret. Every hit, every pain, everything I'd never done or said to anyone, everything that had hurt me that I had just shoved down and buried, left to fester deep inside of me.

In that light, I was pure too.

I was love.

I was breath.

I was free.

I was new, and I was me again, pieced back together and made complete.

It was heaven.

I was home.

The contrast between those feelings and what I'd felt on earth was shocking. I hadn't realized just how much pain I'd been in. I hadn't realized just how much we all have become programmed, desensitized, and disconnected from God's love and light while conforming to how we think we have to be, have to look, and have to act to fit in with everyone else.

We were walking then, my hand in God's like a little kid who just loves feeling loved and connected, as these thoughts and emotions bubbled up in me and blended into the light.

God would see it, too, and lovingly reassure me again that it was going to be okay, like a loving father comforting his child: "It's okay. Everything will be taken care of. Come on. Come with me."

Eventually, I gave in and surrendered. I basked in the love and the light. But after a short time walking together toward something incredible that I could only just sense—for some reason, I glanced down. It was the only time I looked down the entire time. Everything else had been so consuming and wonderful that I didn't think to look around. But when I did, a vision stopped me in my tracks.

That's when I saw my body again, but this time I wasn't on the ice or the stretcher or in the ambulance. I was in a casket that was beginning to be lowered into the ground, and Brooke and our kids were there, all wearing black. She was crying. The kids were crying, and she was rubbing their little backs to comfort them. As the undertaker began his work and my casket began to slowly lower into the ground, I watched my kids throw themselves onto the top of the casket, not wanting to say goodbye. A shovel full of fresh brown dirt hit their backs and showed up muddy on their black suits and dress.

I froze. I could still see myself walking with God, could still feel his hand on mine, but I couldn't erase that vision or ignore the pain that I felt in my kids' hearts.

Before I even told God what I saw, he already knew: "They will all be okay. I promise. You don't have to worry."

But my kids are so young! Four, two, and one—they can't—

And again, God spoke in the most comforting, knowing, reassuring voice: " They will be okay." I could almost feel the warm light smiling and reassuring, with just a tiny bit of sadness at my confusion and concern.

It wasn't an easy decision. Why would I go back to all the stress and the shit of life—the questions and the worries, the fear and the doubts, the pain, the frustrations, the burden, and all that *weight*? How could I? I was free of it *all*. I could take a full, deep, unrestricted breath for maybe the first time in my life. How had I ever breathed before all that weight got taken away?

As I weighed all of this and thought, Can I go back? the answer was clear. I could go back, but I didn't have to. It was my choice. They would be okay. He would take care of them if I wanted to stay.

But I could go back. I had to go back. I had a choice, and there was only one I could make.

I have to go. I have to get back to them.

I still had people in the world who mattered. I had my family to take care of. And God had family for me to take care of, too.

I didn't know how this sort of thing worked, so I just kind of blurted out a bargain: *What can I do to go back? How do I serve you enough to earn it?*

Did I need to sell all my possessions and go on a mission trip or something? Was I supposed to give everything away? I would do anything to get back to my family. I just needed to know.

The response was immediate, before I even vocalized the question, again without any booming voice or audible words. It felt like gentle laughter, reverberating all through my body. And I knew. The instructions I received were so simple and so powerful that I knew I could deliver them to everyone I ever met once I returned back to serve.

"Take this feeling of unconditional love, warmth, and light that you feel right now with me, and share it with every person you come across for the rest of your life. Love them like they are your brothers and sisters. All of them."

I nodded, knowing I could and would live this truth when I went back. How could I ever lose this feeling? How could I live without sharing?

I turned to leave and then looked back once more to ask, "Is there anything else you want me to do?"

With a loving warmth that I will never forget, God said, "Just promise me you will share this."

///

I woke up once in the ambulance, not all at once. It was like waking up slowly on a Sunday morning, when the sun is warm and you still remember a dream. For a few moments, I could still feel the light through my body and the weightlessness of that space that had no space.

"Did you guy see any of that?" I tried to ask, through a jaw I could barely move.

"Sir, you've been in an accident...we're taking you to the hospital...try to relax..."

It couldn't have been more than a minute or two of lingering light and warmth before gravity found me again.

Like a roller coaster bottoming out, I was sucked back into this reality in all of its broken fullness. Not only did the weight come rushing back, and the pain of a broken nose and collarbone and banged up jaw that was out of alignment, but all of the lingering injuries that had stacked up over the years hit me too. All at once, I realized just how much pain I'd been holding and had a sense that there would be much more to come.

There was no way to know just how long the journey ahead of me would be. There was no way to know my career had ended when my life did. There was no way to reconcile the joy I'd felt just moments before with the despair that was waiting for me.

I would get calls to play again. Teams in Russia and Switzerland wanted to talk to me, and I tried to convince myself and others that it would happen. After all, in my heart of hearts, that's really what I wanted. I believed I could wait it out, and the headaches would go away or my memory would come back. After all, every other time I'd been injured, it just...got better.

The first time I got a concussion, I was eleven years old, playing with kids two years older than me. I came around from behind the net to try to score a quick wraparound goal, and a huge defenseman twice my size came around the net and hit me. I didn't see him. He hit me so hard he cracked my helmet right down the middle, and he broke the cage as well. It came down on the bridge of my nose, breaking it for the first time.

When my dad, the coach, and trainer of the team reached me on the ice, I was trying to get my bearings. He asked me if I was okay. Even though I was crying a little, my head was pounding, and my nose was broken, I told him, "Yeah, yeah, I'm good." Because that's how you answer that question. I didn't want to let him down or have him think I wasn't tough.

The second concussion was bad enough that they escorted me off the ice. It was from a dirty check from Tie Domi that got me so squarely I couldn't remember my name. I took a slap shot coming over the Leafs' blue line, and a second later his helmet connected with my temple. Everything went black. It only lasted for fifteen seconds, but I was helped off the ice by my teammates, trainers, and the medical staff. My eyes were twitching sideways. I had no way to pull up information in my mind, and I couldn't stop crying. It was terrifying. And as soon as the trainer saw what was going on, I didn't play another game that season.

But I healed. And I healed again. And again. Over and over, my body and my career seemed to respond as long as I just kept going through the third and fourth, and even that weird one that only mattered enough to hurt my chances of staying with the Predators organization.

So this time, even though I couldn't be around bright lights or handle the noise of my children playing or hang onto short-term memory, if someone asked me how I was, I knew what to say. "Yeah, I'm good. I think I'll go play in Russia. It's not as physical over there...bigger surface, different kind of game..."

I had to, because if people saw what kind of shape I was really in, I wasn't sure what kind of rejections would come my way or how permanent they would be. I had already been professionally blackballed as a "concussion guy," and I saw how tough it could be to get a job again once an injury like that happened. But where do you go when your career is done with you or your friends and family get tired of you? What's the interpersonal version of being sent down?

I had to pretend I was coming back because I was aimless without hockey. I was embarrassed.

And somewhere deep down, I was ashamed that the promise I made to God couldn't be fulfilled. I had no way to talk about it—not only because I didn't feel the love anymore, but because I literally couldn't form my thoughts anymore.

It's one thing to lose your sense of identity when you're still able to think rationally, but when your brain isn't cooperating either, it's like you don't even know who you are at all. Nothing was familiar. Nothing was right.

The injury felt different than any of the others. My future looked different than I ever imagined it could be. My brain was different than I knew it to be. It was all so devastating. It was all so wrong.

It would take me years of anger, pain, suffering, and confusion to finally understand. To realize that it was actually perfect. To realize the light had been with me all along.

Share this love. Share this light.

I had promised I would. It seemed impossible not to. But back in that moment, still consumed and held and loved, I didn't know just how dark it could get.

CHAPTER TEN

THE DARK BEFORE THE DAWN

The deeper I sank into my injury, the more I realized what I had lost. Even the most basic tasks were beyond me. There was a near-constant, stabbing pain in my head behind my eyes, a loss of balance, and no way to sleep. My neck always hurt, and I couldn't get my back stable. I was always uncomfortable. I spent most of my days in bed, hiding from the light and the noise, and my nights in bed with a drink, hoping to relax enough to sleep. But maybe the worst of it all was just how hard it was to get my brain to work.

My memory was inaccessible. It felt like the words and memories I needed to find were filed away in a dusty old library instead of the high-speed internet I was so used to accessing memories with. I'd try to bring a notepad around with me, but then I would forget the notepad or forget that I'd written something helpful in it. There were no easy solutions—no real solutions at all.

Imagine going to the grocery store to get some breakfast ingredients. Your list is simple: bananas, eggs, and milk. But as soon as you walk through the door of the Safeway just around the corner from your house, the list is gone. Not from your hand, but from your mind.

How do you piece it back together?

I couldn't. I knew Brooke was making breakfast and that I was there at the store to help her, but the items escaped me. I shuffled around the dairy and cereal aisles, waiting for something to jog my memory, looking like an old man with dementia—lost, not knowing what was going on.

I called Brooke, who graciously reminded me. *Milk, eggs, bananas.* Then I hung up the phone and walked straight to the milk section to get the jug of milk. As soon as it was in my hands, the other items were lost again. I knew one was close by. I knew she had just told me. And I knew I couldn't access it no matter how hard I tried.

I called her back. There were just two things left: eggs and bananas.

I could do this.

I went straight to the eggs, chanting, "Eggs, eggs, eggs, eggs..." until I got there. But then the third thing was gone again.

I was too embarrassed and hurt to call her a third time, so I just texted instead.

DAVE: I'm sorry. What was the last thing?

BROOKE: Bananas. :(

///

It's terrifying to think back to those years when I couldn't stand to be in the same room with baby cries and shrieks, or when I was physically unable to run with my kids as they learned to ride bikes, or when I couldn't take care of them safely.

A kid crying felt like the sensation we all get with nails on a chalkboard, but to a degree of pain that I can't even describe. Our baby, with his fussiness and screaming, created hours of pain that I couldn't get away from. In one of my lowest moments, we were driving somewhere together when the pain and pressure built and built until I pulled over on the side of the freeway and got out of the car. I felt like I was going insane.

Lower still was the time when Brooke ran to the store and left me in charge of the kids. Of course, they got into some kind of squabble that I had to take care of. Caden was punching his brother, even after I told him no, so I put him in the crib for a little time out. Just two minutes to get him to calm down and teach him not to hit. I kept my composure and thought through what I needed to do.

But when Brooke came home, me and the other kids were out in the pool swimming. When she asked me where Caden was, I couldn't remember.

At all.

It hadn't even registered to me that I needed to look for him. We were in the pool—I should have had my head on a swivel looking for him. But it didn't cross my mind.

As soon as she asked, the pieces came together, and I remembered that Caden was in his crib. He had been in there for an hour and was fast asleep. Not only had I forgotten where he was, but I'd forgotten that I had a third child. My brain had gone from poorly functioning to working against me. Against my family. Could she even leave me with the kids anymore? What if something really bad had happened?

Here I thought I left heaven to come back for my wife and kids, but my messed-up brain and its low level of operation made it a struggle to contribute. I couldn't support my wife and family the way I knew I should, and it made me feel like a burden to everyone in my life.

In just a few years, I'd gone from living the rock-star life to not being able to find myself. I didn't know how long it would last or if it would ever end at all. My body didn't work. My brain didn't work. I had no compelling future. People who knew I couldn't play suggested that I coach, but I couldn't even turn my head side to side to watch the play, much less cope with the bright lights and loud sounds. I couldn't even buy my wife fingernail polish for Christmas because the colors and lights and options overwhelmed me to the point of tears. There's no way I could make real-time game decisions.

The Mayo Clinic ran dozens of tests and treatment protocols, and at first, I tried to trick them. But I was having hundreds of episodes where I'd walk to the fridge or into my office and have no idea what I was doing or how I got there. I was clearly sick and confused and frustrated. Nothing that the clinic could do gave me that sense of relief that I'd gotten after the fourth concussion was treated, and the doctor I'd seen before had gone back to Germany somewhere. I tried to reach out and find him, but he was gone.

And the tests at the clinic made me feel like a complete loser.

I had to remember parts of a story, play games (and keep up with them), sit through cognitive therapy and speech pathology, and do all of the things that people with brain injuries have to do. And I kept failing. I couldn't walk a straight line or remember the three little pigs or do anything that used to be simple. That normal people could do. For someone who had a photographic memory his whole life, I didn't want other people's normal to be my standard. I wanted *my normal.*

Even the doctors would only point to slight improvement and nothing more. They'd say things like, "You're not doing terribly, all things considered." But there were too many days when I'd go through some kind of test that they would say went well the day before, when I didn't even remember being there the day before.

During property renovations here in Arizona, I had contractors working on a koi pond and water features for a total invoice of $80,000. One day I showed up to check on the progress, cut them the check for the full amount, and watched the guy's face change completely.

He graciously told me, "Hey, Dave—you already paid me yesterday."

I couldn't keep track of my renovations, understand contracts, or follow the process of selling my properties. With no sense of recovery in sight and the last livelihood I had on the line, I needed some kind of help to keep me on track.

I received an offer through email to hire a Tony Robbins life coach, with an hour of free coaching. It sounded good to have someone watch my back and make sure I didn't do something stupid.

The coach I reached out to asked me what I wanted to do for the rest of my life. I thought back to that moment just before I came back to my body, and how I was supposed to share that same love that I felt, but I wasn't ready to think that far ahead. So I just told him I would love to help mentor young hockey players who want to make it to the NHL. I also wanted to help people out of suffering so they'd never have to suffer like I was right then.

"I do think you need a coach," he told me, "but I think you need something bigger. You need someone who is playing the game at your level."

On blind faith and with nowhere else to go, I signed up for a $10,000 coaching package with this ex-Marine he recommended—a high-level guy who helped me start working through the mess I was in. When we talked about my goals, I was able to break it down a little further: "I want to help kids. I want to mentor them."

We were getting closer now, and it made him think of a Tony Robbins leadership conference that was coming up. He could get me a discounted ticket price.

When I was seventeen, I borrowed a box set of cassettes on "personal power," but that was the last I'd heard of Tony. And I definitely needed some personal power. The bigger selling point was that all kinds of psychologists, doctors, and coaches would be there too.

The only problem was that it was in San Diego. By that point, we had settled in Phoenix. During the back and forth between Milwaukee and Nashville, then Peoria and St. Louis, we'd kept all of our bigger homes rented out while we rented small homes and apartments near my teams. After the fifth concussion, when it was clear I wasn't going to play for St. Louis anymore, we had a choice to make. And really, it was Brooke's choice to make. I tried to contribute, but I was in so much pain and struggling to keep up with things that I had to trust her judgment.

After she got stuck alone in a Milwaukee winter and then a Peoria winter, with a few scary moments driving in icy storms out in St. Louis, we were ready to be in a warmer place. We loved our Phoenix home, and we were closer to the middle between her family and mine.

Phoenix isn't far from San Diego, but a flight was out of the question and the thought of a drive wasn't much better. There would be a ton of blinding sunlight along the winding trek up the mountains, and even if I got there in one piece, the noise of the event could be too much to take. The trip represented everything I had to avoid to stay out of pain. But I had to get there.

I was a body without a brain, a burden to my family, and a shell of a person. I needed a miracle. If this event wasn't going to fix me, I couldn't imagine anything that would. And that thought was unbearable.

It took eight hours of driving to make a six-hour trip. There was a lot of pulling over, snacking, having quick naps, resting my eyes, and driving again to make it to the event. Slumped over in the reclined seat of my car on a pull-out on the mountain pass, I started to pray. I had nothing else.

I told God, "Listen, man. If this thing doesn't work, I don't think I can live another fifty or sixty years like this, in this condition. I am a shell of the man I used to be.

"If this is the place where miracles are going to happen, then let them happen. But no more messing around. Something has to change. Now."

///

The conference was at a meeting space in a San Diego hotel. Maybe a few hundred people were there, but the room was all noise and lights and intensity, even more than I'd realized it would be. Just getting my lanyard was enough to overwhelm me. I had to step outside and catch my breath before I could handle the event itself.

On my way back in, someone stopped me.

"Dave Scatchard? I'm Tony's brother-in-law, Scott Humphrey. I'm from Vancouver, and I'm a big fan. Have you been to one of these events before? Let me take care of you."

Before I knew it, I was swept up to the section with the Platinum Partners. It cost close to $100,000 to become part of this special group and get access to Tony's public and private events for a year. There were about a hundred of us all in the front couple of rows, where the music was pounding and everyone was into all the movement and energy and hugging and high-fiving.

I sat completely still, just trying not to go nuts. I had to take more breaks, trying to time them between speakers.

Apparently, this was one of the events that his trainers and coaches did, so I was confused and upset that I wouldn't even get to see or hear from Tony Robbins at one of his events. But what happened next became so profound that I didn't even care. There were new ways of thinking that shook me up and tools that changed my life, in line with the kind of thing I'd heard on the tapes years before. But one exercise, in particular, grabbed me and dragged me in deeper than I could have ever expected to go.

We were told to visit the purest version of our souls.

I could see this picture of me at five years old. We were at a campground, and I was wearing a Superman cape that my grandma had made for me. The whole time we were there, I'd run around pretending to fly. In the photo, my dad picked me up into the air, and I stretched my arms out in front of me and my legs behind. I smiled at the camera, and they snapped the picture so that it looked like I was flying.

That part came easily enough. That was the David I needed to get to. That pure little soul who loved animals and people and was so joyful and happy...but he was somewhere stuck in this broken, scared, confused man.

As clear as he was in my mind, I couldn't even find a glimmer of that first version of me. All I could see inside was this killer athlete who'd made all the money and gotten all the stuff but couldn't even play with his kids.

The people leading the exercise knew this wouldn't be easy. They said if we couldn't get to that version of ourselves, then we should pull the layers back that kept us from it. We had to actually reach onto our chests and physically pull, like we were removing emotional and psychological layers of armor and masks that were keeping us from it.

Maybe others were just going through the motions, or maybe they'd done it before and it wasn't a big deal, but this was new to me. I couldn't walk away knowing that there was nothing in me but stone and armor. The light had gone out of me. Nothing was left.

I started seeing the layers, which were thin at first. Little moments that hurt my young empathetic heart—the first time my dad, my best buddy, gave me a spanking or my mom grabbed the wooden spoon. The first time a principal yelled at me. The first time I was bullied. The first time I had my heart broken. The first time I lied to a trainer and said I was good to go when my body was screaming at me to stop, and the countless times after that too. Each little hurt needed a new piece of armor so it wouldn't hurt my heart and soul as much. So it wouldn't get in the way of me and my dreams.

In the exercise, which really became a powerful tool for me, I kept going back and forth between the purest version of me— that bright little David skating around with my loving family all around—and the concussed, broken mess sitting in the back of a conference room, weeping.

Terrified that I still couldn't find little David, I thought harder. I dug deeper. The armor was a layer of concrete and metal plating that was extremely heavy and thick, blocking away layers of light and vibration and vulnerability and joy that I'd once had.

I tried to remember, to connect to that part of me who was connected to everyone and everything and felt everything and loved so damn much, but that little light was gone. That part of me was completely turned off so that I felt nothing at all.

The more I looked for little David and couldn't find him, the more I panicked.

For the first time, I saw myself as I truly was: this pillar of armor and stone, so completely covered that I couldn't find my true self anymore. I couldn't get centered because I had no idea where "center" was for me. Thirty-plus years of pain had turned me into something unrecognizable. Decades of going to work every day to play as physical as possible and sometimes hurting people. Decades of ignoring my body's signals, of ignoring my impact on others, of pushing through for one more game, one more fight, one more paycheck.

I had become the gladiator, and there was no arena left for me to fight in.

The "purest version of myself" exercise was long over while I stayed in the back corner of the room, sweating and crying and frantically trying to peel back the layers. I thought of the firefighters I'd met at ground zero, with their bleak faces and aching spirits. How they kept digging and kept working in case just one more person could be found. I had to keep digging. I pulled back layer after layer of hurt and pain and callousness until I felt surrounded by rubble, with little David somewhere inside just waiting to be found.

And then he was there. I was there. I was *there* again—in that exact same vibration of energy and love that I'd felt when I left my body so many months before. As I physically leaned over and picked up this little light of a boy, I reconnected with who I really was and what I was about. I looked down at this angel as I held him, and I found myself. I knew instantly that my life would never be the same again, and I began to tap into that. As I did, it felt like a waterfall of light, of pure grace and love showering down on me from above. As it poured over my naked, vulnerable, true body, I felt like I was being cleansed and freed of all the trauma, pain, and injuries. I felt a surge of energy overflowing through every cell in my body. It felt like everything I had been created to be, finally free of the masks and filters and rubble and armor that weren't me at all. It felt like I'd been suffocating under all those layers and didn't even realize it.

I held little David in my arms and saw my tears dropping onto his face.

I apologized to him. "I didn't mean to bury you like that. Underneath all the armor and masks, suffocating you."

I saw him as part of me again. "You're the best version of me. You're the way that God made me to be."

I acknowledged what I'd done to lose him. "You couldn't have done those things that I just had to do."

And I let go of all the stories and lies for the hope of wholeness. I let go of all the masks and armor and anything I used to protect myself from the pain because I knew that the light glowing around me would protect me for the rest of my life. You can call it blind faith, trust, or surrendering control. Call it whatever you like, but it was powerful!

"It'll never happen again. You're going to lead the way. We are going to be completely open and vulnerable for the world to see because nobody can *not* love you. You'll be protected but not lost. I promise."

The certainty in the way that I said that reminded me of God promising me that everything was going to be okay. It had been three long years spent wondering why I'd left that place. Wondering why God forgot about me and left me in my own darkness. I had been unable to share my love with the world because I was still trying to stop my own pain and suffering. I was unable to share anything with the world because I hadn't been able to find it again for myself.

Until that moment—on my knees, crying in the back of a conference room—I had no idea that the guilt of not being able to help others when I couldn't help myself during those difficult times had been there in me, part of me, all along.

For the first time since I died on the ice and was given my greatest comeback, I could breathe.

I held up that brilliant little version of me and saw God in him. In me. And the second I agreed to let that version of me lead the way, that purest David from so long ago, all of the bound-up energy inside of me, instantly became unbound. It simultaneously exploded into me and out of me, just like I'd experienced in heaven, like an expansion into the next phase of my life. Then all of that grace and love and intuition and creativity came blasting back to me. Everything that had been buried was vulnerable and exposed, yet still safe and warm and loved. The gladiator could rest. The child was finally free.

CHAPTER ELEVEN

COACHED TOWARD COACHING

X

"I'm going to get better, Brooke. I know it."

I had gone to San Diego looking for a miracle, and God had delivered. Twice.

The day after I went looking through the rubble of my own life to find myself again, we had another long session full of speaking and psychological tools and exercises. One of them was called a swish pattern. Riding high from the night before, I listened closely to the instructions and gave it my absolute all.

The goal was to work on things like career and finance, and they asked us to visualize something we were unhappy with and then something that represented what we'd rather be—a future state or a memory of that better state. As hard as I tried, all I could think of was that crumpled image of my body on the ice as I left it to go meet God. So I went with it.

I tried to find the opposite of that broken, tired, empty body on the ice, and I caught a glimpse of blonde frosted hair in a mirror. Eighteen-year-old me, free of so many of the injuries, strong and lean, happy, and with so much life ahead of him.

Then the exercise really began. We homed in on each image as clearly as we could and projected them into our mind's eye. For me, I visualized a huge stained-glass window with my image projected onto it. Then we identified the sound that each image had attached to it as well. When I pictured my broken body, I groaned with the pain I'd felt for so long. When I switched that image with my younger, healthier, happier self, I cheered like I'd just scored a goal. Then the trainer had us switch them back and forth, faster and faster—moving, yelling, groaning. Seeing the images come closer and clearer. Getting so consumed in the images that they felt real and strong and flashing back and forth between the images faster and faster and faster...*crash!* We mentally annihilated that pattern, seeing it explode into flames, evaporating into the air with smoke. Or in my case, I shattered the negative image into a million pieces by throwing a boulder through the stained-glass window, with only the positive image remaining.

You're interrupting brain patterns that have been used so long they're automatic, engrained in us as our reality, when in fact, they're just an altered perception of reality. We replace them with something new. Making it so you think of your body as the young and fit version, not the old and broken one. And it worked. I got so supercharged with the energy of yelling and moving and visualizing that I imagined grabbing a rock and shattering that window into a million pieces that could never be brought back together. I couldn't use that vision anymore. Then I proudly brought the new vision to the front of my mind, and I anchored it with celebration. I yelled and cheered— and something popped.

Just behind my left eye, I felt a release that started to create a spraying sensation, like a hot water bottle that was spraying fluid behind my eye. At first, I was scared, but then the pain started to subside. The pressure that had built up for three years was releasing—*finally* releasing.

I wanted to keep celebrating, but my partner looked up from his exercise and got worried. "Dude, what is wrong with your *face*?"

The trainers and leaders started to freak out, too. From my left temple and eye down to my neck, the whole side of my face where I'd just felt that release had begun to turn purple. They wanted to call an ambulance. I felt incredible. The pressure behind my eye kept draining and draining until it melted away, and I started to remember what it was like to live without all that pain. This was my second miracle.

The moments of deep emotion and discovery and raw vulnerability would come and go, but the pressure didn't come back, and all that I found in those moments stayed with me. All weekend, it felt like I was in a constant conversation with God—like I had gone looking for him, and now he was after me. Like he had something to tell me.

Of all places, he found me while I was looking in the mirror brushing my teeth that night—another miracle that made every dime, every mile, every doubt worth it.

With a voice and a message so clear that I couldn't deny it, I listened intently as God began to speak to me while looking at me through my own eyes. First, with pain in his voice, he said that he was sorry that I had to suffer so long, but there was a reason for it.

He gently explained that I had to suffer, scrape, and feel the pain of living in a dark pit, feeling hopeless and confused with no compelling future, no identity, and no idea how I was going to get myself out of this place. I needed to understand what anxiety, depression, darkness, and desperation felt like because the people who were going to be coming to me would be coming from this place. I could now show them how to climb out of this pit of hell and get back to living like a champion again. I could understand firsthand what they were going through.

He was looking right at me through my own eyes, and I could tell that he loved me. But there was a sadness there too. Something deeply hurt about all that pain I felt. Something that knew all of this was going to have to happen before I could do what I came back to do—that I had to know what darkness felt like in order to reach people who were still stuck in it.

Not all of my pain, confusion, and memory went away that weekend. But it did start to subside. I was able to finish the conference. I was able to *slowly* get back into the gym and *slowly* research the programs Tony had to offer, including a $20,000 Mastery University course in Palm Springs, California. It included Date with Destiny, Life Mastery, and Wealth Mastery.

I originally planned on doing the Mastery University alone, but a friend recommended the full Platinum Partnership. It was expensive—by the time you added up travel, hotels, and the platinum membership, you were looking at over $100,000. But I loved what I was seeing already, and I just knew that I needed to do it. I wouldn't be able to explain it to Brooke or convince her, so I just had to go with the calling inside of me and join.

That program gave me an all-access pass to almost any event he put on around the world for the next year, as well as a few private events with just Tony, Sage, and the Platinum Partners. My newfound status put me right back in the front row for even more life-changing events.

A couple of days into my first event as a Platinum Partner, Tony led us in some chakra visualizations that he'd learned from India. Opening with a gong and some calming music, he guided us through each color of the chakra, moving up through different parts of the body. He had us picture it radiating out from ourselves and through the conference room, spreading through the hotel and across the town, and filling up the state, country, and world. Our focus was on breath and visualization and nothing else.

When we got to the heart chakra, I imagined this green light shooting out from my chest with the same vibration of love and gratitude I felt in heaven, and my body started to respond. I became lightheaded, which I attributed to the breathing pattern. I was seated next to a guy named Chad Wohlers, who's now a great friend of mine, and later he said he tried to match my breathing pattern but couldn't. I cycled through the one-two, one-two breaths that we were guided to do, and a much slower breath that felt like a minute of inhalation and just as long to exhale began taking over. But then I felt a humming sensation as well.

My body started to tingle and vibrate, starting from the root chakra in my tailbone and radiating up—like it was brewing underneath me and trying to work its way up to the spine. As the vibrations grew stronger, my hands started to bounce up and down on my quads. I couldn't stop any of it. The vibrations grew higher, and the energy moved so strongly through me that it began pushing me off my seat. My body felt controlled by this energy, slapping my knees and jerking around, and I wanted to try to stop it. But when I tried to stand up, it was like a force slammed me back down. The pressure held me down in my chair—it was a strong but loving message that *I'm not done with you yet*.

I could feel people staring at me, though I couldn't open my eyes. Just like before, Tony had long since moved on, and I was still stuck in the power of the exercise. I couldn't stop it, so I just let it ride out.

Unfortunately, someone thought I was having a seizure.

Someone reached around from behind me and stuck something sugary in my mouth. The people around me cleared out, and trainers started to come check on me. And still, I couldn't stop whatever was happening to me.

Honestly, I think there was something about that higher frequency that was trying to do its job. But there was so much damage that my body was hanging onto that it wasn't an easy process.

I was able to tell the trainers to "hang on, hang on—it's almost done," more than ready for that to be true. The regular programming of the event was back on, and Tony was back on stage teaching again, but I couldn't stop vibrating. My body just had energy surging through it, but I knew God was working on me and this was a gift for me to absorb. I was drenched in sweat and starting to cry...when these arms wrapped around my chest from behind. He leaned his bearded cheek on my face and just breathed with me. The second he wrapped me up, everything in me exhaled and softened.

It felt like Jesus was holding me.

"Thank you, brother."

"No problem," he said, and didn't let go. "You went pretty deep, huh?"

The man with the beard was another Platinum Partner from Brazil. His name was Eli, and he told me that he does spiritual work and that what I was going through was familiar to him. He knew exactly what was happening to me. At one point, I heard him tell the others around me to back off because I was in the middle of a spiritual experience.

In another exercise utilizing *om* chanting, I felt a rush of heat go from my tailbone to the top of my head. The heat brought pressure, which encircled my head like the beginnings of a migraine, growing stronger and stronger until I thought I might pass out. I stepped back to a wall to steady myself, and then it all released at once. With it, something else shifted in my body. It felt like something opened up that had been locked before—not just a spiritual awakening, but part of the healing after my concussions.

Seizing, shaking, and vibrating at a higher frequency with more intensity than I ever imagined possible and being held by a strange Brazilian man: this is what the seminars were like for me, fourteen to sixteen hours a day, for seven days straight.

I ended up going to bed that night thoroughly exhausted, spent but the most relaxed I had felt in years. The tension that I had carried within my body for years was gone, almost like it was in heaven. As I lay on my bed that night, completely naked, I whispered to God, "If there is anything left, you may as well get it now."

I chuckled, but then I felt another wave that had me fully vibrating again for another four or five minutes. It felt like for each and every hit that my body had taken over my lifetime as a hockey player, it was trying to fix it and realign everything to the way it was. After that, I passed out and slept hard. When I woke up, I was completely recharged and ready to go see what crazy stuff was going to happen next.

///

As much as I absorbed the energy of the exercises, I also observed Tony like I had observed the pros as a kid. I learned his patterns and processes so that by the end of the week I could almost always tell where he was going with each new intervention. I took notes to remember every turn of phrase, every question he would ask. I learned how he led people to unearth their belief system and model of the world—never just telling them the answer, but asking things like, "Whose love did you crave the most as a child?" and "What do you think is stopping you?" I followed along as he moved them from their beliefs to how those things influence their actions and how they could use all of that to move forward.

And that was just the first week.

Across the whole Platinum Partnership year, we covered business mastery, leadership, health, wealth, and everything you can think of. I went all in for every category.

After being so strict about my diet for training when I was playing in the NHL, when I retired, I told myself that I could take my foot off the gas. At first, it was a treat, but then I lost a lot of discipline. I could enjoy any food I wanted for the first time since I was a kid. With no compelling future, why would I need to be in shape? I couldn't work out anyway, so what was the point? I couldn't stop.

Now that I was in Tony's world, I was really changing my ways. I quickly went vegan and stopped drinking until a vacation to Cabo broke my sixty-five-day streak. I think that time helped to detoxify my body not only of the physical trauma but of the food and alcohol choices I had made since the injury.

With the coaching and events, Platinum Partnership also included three trips to places all around the world. The first flight was to India since a lot of his philosophies and mediation skills and techniques came from the people at the Oneness University.

I was open to it all, and it was a lot to take in. The crazy taxi ride, the bizarre traffic patterns, everyone honking their horns, and so many people everywhere. A couple of other attendees and I decided to go souvenir shopping before the event started, and the tuk-tuk that we hailed to get there almost killed us.

If you've never seen a tuk-tuk, it's like a motorized rickshaw, with open sides where you sit. He wasn't *actually going to kill us*. For him, it was totally normal. But missing cars by inches, driving the wrong way, turning on reds when it didn't make sense, and beeping everywhere...that felt anything but normal. There was some kind of flow to it, some way of communicating with horns that I couldn't decipher, but to us, it just looked like we were going to crash any second.

We spent time in Chennai with Oneness University, where Tony put on an incredible show, as always. The gorgeous facility, which I'd really just call a temple, had amazing tents set up outside that held elephants, acrobats, and all kinds of beautiful sights to rival any Cirque du Soleil-type performance. But the grounds themselves were just as breathtaking, in a peaceful kind of way. It's no wonder people come from all over the world to train there with the monks for weeks and months at a time, sometimes for their whole lives. It was so easy to tune in and experience visions there.

Later, we took a private plane to one of the holiest of the seven sacred cities in Hinduism, Varansi. There, we visited the Ganges River, which the locals called Mother. We were told that they believe everyone was created from that river and that they had to make it back there in death as well. So the banks of the Ganges in Varansi are always filled with pilgrims who have brought their dead to be cremated on the river banks. The remains of what's left after burning are floated through the river, and the banks are piled with logs that are taller than most of the buildings, so they're always ready for constant burning.

The mixture of beautiful sacred beliefs and overwhelming pollution and filth was jarring. Walking along, we watched as a little boy found a human limb that had fallen off of a fire and ran to put it back to finish the cremation. Someone else drove by with a cart carrying a body, with a head dangling out.

While the devout belief was fascinating, it had also polluted this once-beautiful river so much that it could barely sustain life. The ritual of death has consumed it entirely. Yet people are so moved by what they believe it to be that they jump into it when they see it, trying to wash and clean themselves and fill themselves with the goddess—unable to see that it is filled with bodies and filth.

And as bizarre as the scene was for us, we stood out like a sore thumb to them too. With all 6'7" of Tony, most of us Caucasian, and TV cameras all around, we couldn't go anywhere without a swarm of people following us. Two of us got separated from the group and a little bit lost, and a local came up to us offering a blessing. He spoke some words over us and put the red bindi on our foreheads—then asked for fifty bucks. I guess, like anywhere in the world, some of the deepest beliefs are polluted just as much as the Ganges River.

///

One of Tony's strengths is bringing people in from all kinds of spiritual and philosophical backgrounds. There was no preaching or anything that felt forced, and you could always sit out if something felt uncomfortable. Of course, I've never been one to avoid discomfort. Most of us stayed through all of it.

There was the typical Tony Robbins training around mindset and limiting belief systems, but the others were even more fascinating. A laughing monk who was so genuinely joyful that he laughed all the time. A series of open-eyed blessings that felt vulnerable and powerful. A daily deep-dive meditation led by some monks from Oneness University. And thanks to some meditative practice I had done at home leading up to the trip, I was able to settle into the sessions and lose track of time.

After coming out of each meditation, a coach walked each of us up to the stage, where the monk would pray for us and give us a blessing. In that one-on-one moment, the monk held each person's head in his hands, with each hand on their head, wrapping over the top of their ears. We watched the monk perform this on dozens of people, and he taught us how to do a Deeksha blessing ourselves.

There was always a beautiful feeling of calm that washed over you after the Deekshas. The fight-or-flight response almost turned off, and the survival part of the brain felt quiet. It felt like the blessing reached that part of my brain, soothing the parts of me that had been on high alert for so long.

Even without the blessings, the meditations were intensely healing. My subconscious was dealing with so much that I hadn't been able to process yet. After two hours at a time of that completely open state, I was totally blissed out every time.

Near the end of one of these meditations, I had a vision of myself being in utero again and then re-birthed in a peaceful way. I envisioned resting on my mother's stomach and holding onto her, telling her how sorry I was for almost killing her. My birth had not been easy—breech and twenty-eight hours long. She must have told me a thousand times, "You know you almost killed me giving birth to you, right?" But in that moment, I could feel this rush of healing. I don't know if it was for me or for her, but it was full and complete. When they came to get me for my blessing, I was the last one in the room.

In an odd and sweet moment in time, the monk rested his hands on my head and sighed. I don't know what he saw, but he reacted with an *awww* sound, almost like he could feel that I had been cracked open. Then he prayed for me, and we ended the session.

In another meditation—this one back at Oneness University—we sat in a circle with our eyes closed. As the breathing pattern and exercise progressed, my body felt like I was swept up into a tornado. I swirled higher and higher, looking down on the group from above until it felt like we all swirled together into one connection. When the coach came to grab me, I realized I was once again sitting alone in a large group of chairs in the circle, and because of how deep I was in the meditation, the monks left me for last again. When they came to get me for my blessing, I still felt connected to the others, but no one was around me anymore at all.

One of the other aspects of the training was that daily we would be led through this movement class nicknamed trance dancing. It was led by a beautiful young lady named Lucia. She came from the 5Rhythms family in Hawaii, and she was supposed to lead us in trance dancing. About a hundred of us filed into the room awkwardly. She told us there was no pressure—we were just going to walk around to the music playing in the background.

Before long, we had settled into a counterclockwise pattern, walking around and around in a circle. Lucia laughed. "I said to walk around, but I never said anything about walking in a circle!"

Because of the way our culture craves alignment, we follow each other. We assume there's some kind of rule, and we align to it, even if we can't put our finger on it exactly. So we moved stiffly and put ourselves into a box, or in this case a circle, of familiar patterns. Those boxes give us the "certainty" that we are doing it right and being good boys and girls—until Lucia stopped the music and encouraged us to loosen up.

She asked, "Do you mind if I show you what the human body is capable of when it lets go of inhibitions and just moves to the music?"

I've never seen a human being move with the grace and fluidity that she had. The whole room fell silent watching her flow and move to the beautiful music she turned on. When the music stopped, we stayed silent for a long beat before erupting in a cheer. We were amazed.

She wanted us to do *that*. Us, this group of people who could afford our Platinum Partnership membership—doctors, lawyers, scientists, entrepreneurs, coaches. Most of the group was very cerebral people who weren't really physical or present in their bodies. "This is what can happen when you let the soul be the soul, without any rules."

She dimmed the lights so that we would feel less exposed and then started the music up again. I started by weaving around upstream, the opposite direction of everyone else. For all of the meditation and things we'd done just inside our heads, it felt amazing to be present in my body again. At one point, I squatted down on the ground, envisioning myself as a caveman, just organically banging the backs of my hands against the carpeting of the conference room, imagining a huge bonfire in front of me. It was a primal feeling, and Lucia encouraged me to keep moving with it.

Each day, we'd come back to the trance dance class, and each day I would go deeper and deeper. I morphed from a caveman into the world's greatest ballet dancer, flying around the conference room with my eyes closed, like it was a meditation in itself. I felt like a bird flying through a canyon. I felt like I could jump in the air and float across the room. I spun like a whirling dervish and ran and leaped and lost all awareness of my body.

And I never once ran into another person.

When that realization hit me, it was followed quickly by another: What if our way isn't the only way?

What if we're guided, every step of the way? What if we can become so connected that we feel each other even when we can't see? Maybe that's why the tuk-tuk can drive the wrong way down the street and fly around corners without hitting any other vehicles. Maybe that's why they could worship so many gods when America is so tied to just one. Maybe that's why the river can be death and life all at once. What if all of the programming that we follow in circles isn't all that there is?

What if I removed all of those limitations from my world?

I wanted to test it.

I backed up to one side of the room and started to pray. *God, if you're up there, guide me through this room filled with people.*

Keep me safe. Keep everyone safe. Don't let me hit anybody while I dance like a crazy person without opening my eyes until I reach the other side of the room.

With blind faith, I closed my eyes and took off.

Sometimes I was spinning. Sometimes I was jumping. I was sideways and backward and around in circles. I began to feel the people around me like I was slipping into their energy, and I could avoid them even when I moved really quickly. Clips of the movie *The Matrix* came to mind as I swirled and ducked and slipped in and out of energy, just missing people and them just missing me. When I made it through the field of people, I reach out my right hand, opened my eyes, and was touching the other wall over 100 feet from where I began.

I had made it, only because I had been guided.

Lucia stopped the music and told the class, "Dave's got it. And you've got more. Let go."

The floor cleared out, and I went for it again. I danced as hard and as crazy as I could, flowing with the music and keeping my eyes shut the whole time. I whipped my hat off my head and threw it into the air. I spun and jumped and moved, vaguely hearing a little chuckling around me in the background. It wasn't until the song was over that I found out I had broken the chandelier that was hanging from the tall ceiling above me when I threw my hat, and crystals were dropping to the ground around me without hitting me.

At the end of these dances, I felt like I'd been in a massage rather than movement. It was like all of the blocks, all of the things I tried to control, everything had been released. I started to think about just how much capacity that gave me now that I was becoming free. How much magic and healing I had at my fingertips.

///

I don't pretend to know what's really going on in any of those spaces. All I know is that I felt lighter, buzzing with energy and freedom each time a new part of myself was unearthed. One monk explained that my body was shaking and vibrating in those exercises because the injuries in my body were blocking the flow up and down my spine. Until those were healed, it had to work around all of the knocks and shifts and brokenness. Another told me that I had the capacity to harness the energy but not to use it yet, so it would literally take over my body.

Later, I heard the theory that the more trauma a person has early in their life, the more that pure childhood energy gets bound up and stuck in their body. If that's true, then the work that I had to do to cultivate energy to get to the NHL and stay there, after years of injuries and bullying and separation and loss, became a trauma in itself. All of that together had been bound up inside of me for my whole life. By working with people who are immersed in that kind of work, we could begin to unwind and unlock everything that had been stuck inside of me for so long.

There was one hilarious moment from another seminar where I stood in a room full of coaches, all in their own broken states of healing and growth just like I was in, and found myself working with a new partner because both of ours had stepped away. We moved through an anchoring and mirroring exercise together, and suddenly he was telling me about his childhood. I put my hand on his shoulder, and it felt like a current of electricity connected us. I talked to him, just like when I was brushing my teeth and felt God talking to me.

He broke down sobbing as the message flowed through me and into this guy I'd never met before. He looked at me with tears in his eyes and said, "I've been in therapy for this my whole life, and you just changed everything for me in five minutes. How long have you been coaching?"

By then, our partners came back, wondering what was happening with both of us bawling and holding each other.

"Oh, I'm not a coach at all." I laughed, wiping his snot off my shirt and sniffing at my own. I looked up and around the room, laughing at the wonder of it all. Feeling giddy and silly, I said, "We've just got some God stuff happening here," and I shot my arm up at a burned-out light near us, goofing off in a *let there be light*, Thor-like kind of motion. But the freaking light flickered on! We all looked at each other in shock and then burst out in laughter and wonder, smiling from ear to ear.

Can you see why these are stories I don't often tell? They're hard to make sense of. They're hard to believe or explain or understand. They're funny and miraculous, intense, and freeing.

Whatever was happening during those events, coming back home was always like going to a new planet. Even in the abject poverty that surrounded each location we visited in India, there was such joy in the people we saw. Kids would be out playing stick ball or cricket in their underwear, dodging stagnant water and trash, yet still so incredibly happy. Not only did I feel more gratitude for what I had at home, but I became frustrated with the excess of it.

It was difficult to hold the tension between excess and the way the universe wants us to be abundant. I learned I could actually hustle harder *and* play harder. To bring value to people and make more money. As long as it was all wrapped up in immense gratitude and an urgency to have an impact and help humanity, it could work.

Nothing could shake that gratitude either. That trip gave me the fundamentals of healing and focus that would carry me into the next stage of life. I drank up everything that they could teach me until it became second nature.

I would get teary-eyed seeing my kids healthy, even if they were fighting. I'd find myself saying things like, "Don't they have beautiful lungs? Listen to how powerful their lungs are!"

My life was clearly changing. I stayed close to Tony so that I could continue to learn from him. He kept introducing new healers and leaders to our group, and I would just dive in headfirst with them as well. I felt this could keep me close to that space that I had uncovered. I signed up for the Platinum Partnership again for a second year. I did everything he told me to do.

So after months of work, sitting in the front row of another event, I was shocked to hear Tony call me out. Standing in front of me, with a couple thousand people behind: "And you," he said. "Shame on you, Dave."

Uh...what? What do you mean, I thought. I'm just here to learn and enjoy the night, man!

"Shame on you for not helping all those people who need you right now."

Oh, shit.

"Fuck you for being so selfish. There are thousands of people who need your help, and you're waiting around until you're *better* or you're *trained* or you've figured it all out. Fuck you. People need you right now. Save somebody's life. Stop being selfish. It's bigger than you and your stuff."

Oh, God. He's right.

Healing is messy work. At first, I had to pull out pieces of the dead gladiator that had rotted inside of me. I had to work so hard to protect that child inside of me, and I thought I couldn't put on armor ever again without losing him. I thought the only way to stay safe was to meditate five hours a day and stay away from everything I had known before.

Tony talked to me again after that event and said, "Look, you're like a monk in your cave. Who are you helping other than yourself?"

It wasn't exactly the way God had talked to me, but the message was the same. I had come back to help people, but my newfound state seemed so fragile. I was so sensitive to slipping in and out of this open state I'd discovered that I only felt safe when I was hidden. I would step into the theater room in my house, shut the lights off, and do my meditation work all alone. Brooke could tell that I was healing, but she didn't quite understand the methods. And I didn't understand how to integrate them into life. Not yet.

The hard truth is that it's almost as easy to be a monk as it is to be a gladiator. It's facing challenges while remaining vulnerable that's the real work. I had to learn that not all armor is bad. There were pieces of it—courageousness, boldness, action, relentlessness, determination—that I could scrounge back up and use when I needed them.

I learned to physically reach down and put on the armor when something seemed especially scary or challenging and then take it off as soon as I crushed that obstacle. The things that got me from the coal town to the NHL weren't all bad—I just didn't need to carry it all around at the same time.

///

When the second year's Platinum subscription rolled around, I went in with a mission. Instead of watching the interventions and feeling entertained, I studied Tony. I wrote down every moment of every interaction, basically transcribing what Tony was saying as well as how and why and when he said it. I picked up on the neurolinguistic programming that he used as well as the storytelling and communication tactics he used to complete each intervention. I made it my objective to spot his key words, tone, tempo, body language, and physiology that he used and that he got the client to use in order to create transformation.

I modeled my coaching journey after Tony like I modeled my early hockey game after first-round draft picks. You have to follow the people who are playing bigger than you. I learned from healers and monks and shamans. I learned from physical trainers and coaches. I sat in their presence and absorbed their wisdom and expertise just like I sat behind the glass with the older kids and watched my hockey idols shoot the puck over and over again. I read their books and followed their rituals like I bought the same sticks as my idols and skated like they skated.

Incredibly, the more I modeled these heroes of mindset and power and change, the more I heard my dad in them. He was such a trailblazer without even realizing what he was doing.

Dad was one of the first guys in Canada to jump off a mountain hang-gliding, with the sixth license for hang-gliding that Canada ever gave out. After showing everyone else it was possible, he started a club for the others who wanted to experience that thrill too. He barefoot water-skied, drove motorcycles, and coached hockey even though he hadn't played. He didn't see the limits that other people saw.

He was the dad who would tell me to jump higher if I wanted to nail that trampoline backflip, not the typical "you'll break your neck" caution that other parents might give. He let us kids race canoes on the lake even though it took hours. He let me ride my BMX bike all over town without restrictions or limits. He was strict about the rules that he did have, but he didn't like them to be arbitrary.

Don't lie; don't cheat; don't steal. Tell the truth and help people, and you'll be free to find the life you want to live.

He never once told me I couldn't make it to the NHL, but he did give me a book called *Many Are Called, Few Are Signed* so that I could know just how stacked the odds were against me. He was honest about the work that I'd have to do if I wanted to reach my goals, and then he stood beside me while I did that work.

One summer after I'd been in the NHL a couple of years, we all went out on the lake like old times. Sitting on the shore together and looking out over the water, I said, "I wonder how far it is to that other shore. Maybe a couple miles?"

"I don't know," he mused back, sipping a beer.

It was quiet for a few more moments before my thoughts slipped out again: "Do you think I could swim across there?"

He smiled and said again, "I don't know."

Without saying another word, I walked into the lake and started swimming. A few minutes later, my dad appeared behind me in the canoe, making sure I was safe from any boat traffic and making extra sure that he was there to encourage me along the way. He never told me I couldn't. He never said to stop or told me to change course. Just stayed there beside me, letting me know he was there and he believed in me.

After what seemed like a couple of hours, I made it to the other bank and turned around to go back. When I did, I felt a strong current pushing me forward—the same current I'd been swimming against without realizing it.

About a quarter of the way back across, exhausted and with so far left to go, my dad offered a quiet reminder: "You just said you'd try to swim across. You didn't mention anything about swimming back."

Feeling accomplished, exhausted, and supported as always, I climbed into the canoe, and we headed back for the evening, laughing at what had just transpired.

That was life with my dad, from beginning to end. When I was nine years old, he had me doing visualization exercises. If I couldn't get to the rink to skate, he taught me to go up to my room, close my eyes, and run through an entire practice or game situation. I didn't realize exactly what was happening then, but now those kinds of meditation practices fill my coaching sessions. I can take people where they want to be or take them through experiences I've had, even to heaven with me, so that they can experience the vibrations of love and healing and abundance that they want to access.

He also had me writing out goals from a young age, just like I coach people to do now. When I was fifteen, I wrote out that I wanted to marry a model who was kind and loving. I wanted three kids—two boys and a girl. I wanted pets and a mansion with a koi pond. I wanted a Dodge Stealth—the exact car that I got just a few years later. I wanted to make a million dollars, score a goal in the NHL, and play for at least three years.

A few years ago, I found that list again and couldn't believe how accurate it was to my life. Every single day, I'm living out the dream that teenage me could only imagine. Thanks to my dad, I believed in those dreams enough to make them my reality.

///

The wisdom my dad carried didn't always look like softness and light—not until his last year on earth.

The year before he passed, he had an accident while ice fishing.

While he never talked about what happened when he went under, he did offer that he knew what I'd been talking about all those years. I can't help but believe that what he experienced was similar to what I did. I think he saw the other side too—and he completely changed overnight. I think back now to all of the things that he said to me that last summer that he never said before, and I wonder if his time was up, except for one more visit back to let us know how much he loved us.

Even though he had always been supportive and believing and hopeful, his own dad had never modeled real unconditional love to him. All of those visionary tendencies he had were wrapped up in a hard-ass exterior, and it melted away after that accident. All that was left was grateful, loving support. He hugged me that summer and didn't let go. He just held me and held me, like I used to do with him. He told me how proud he was of me and how I was such a good kid. He told me how beautiful my family was and what a good dad I had become. He told me how much he loved me and gave me a hug that lasted longer than normal.

Those were the last words he ever spoke to me.

After working himself to the bone our whole lives, I think he had done all the work he was supposed to do here. He even went out the way he would have wanted to. He died of an aortic aneurysm a month later, while bringing my mom a coffee in bed the day after he played eighteen holes of golf.

It has taken my whole life to mirror the kind of belief in people that my dad had. He just didn't see negative—it wasn't in his vocabulary. He only saw the bright side of challenges. He always had a smile on his face and never talked down about people or players. Every struggle was an opportunity to help someone see things differently. The catch was that he actually believed those words, and in his last times on earth, we could see that belief completely unchained. I was so lucky to have him in my corner my whole life.

The psychology of positivity works wonders—to a certain degree. Back in gladiator mode, when I was buried under all of that armor, I reflected my dad's positivity and belief without living in their vibration. My instinct was to say, "I'm good," even when my shoulder had been ripped out of its socket or I was swimming in a post-concussion fog. I struggled to find the words for my deep depression even as it tried to take over my whole life.

In order to truly tap into the real gifts that are around you, to respond to the nudges that the universe is giving you, you have to get down to your true, authentic self. You can't tell yourself lies anymore. You have to face reality in order to move beyond it.

That's not an easy thing to do when we have to be honest about all of our hurts and darkness and pain. But when we really take in everything around us and become grateful for it, the little things add up to an overwhelming sense of joy. I became grateful for the way the sun rises and the way freshly cut grass smells. For the little things my kids would do or the small progress I could make in a workout.

Then it began to snowball—I became grateful that my mom was able to give me a call or that my body could move to pick up the phone. I was grateful for the electricity and signal that made the call happen. For the glass in my cabinet and running water that I filled it with while my mom told me about her own beautiful, normal day.

Gratitude began to pour out of me in ways that I never experienced while living out my dreams with all the money and fans and famous friends. Those things were fun, and they were a bonus part of my amazing life, but they didn't bring me joy like I've found in celebrating the miracle of existence itself.

My dad felt that joy. He saw potential in people more than they could see in themselves. He believed in them more than they could believe in themselves. He saw their souls, not their roles. All along, my dad was teaching me that the only thing you don't want to be is *the same as everyone else*. Why settle for okay when extraordinary is available? Why keep up with the

Joneses when rock star shit is just around the corner? Why sit on the sidelines when you can run the whole game?

In India, Shri Bhagavan was asked the secret to happiness, and he told Tony and our entire Platinum Partnership group what my dad lived out every single day: the secret to life is "loving the what-is."

Not what was. Not what's going to happen. But being in love with the moment and everything it holds.

Out of the entire universe and its billions of people, you've been matched with this group of friends and family and mentors and mentees and circumstances. Somehow you're there to serve them, and they're here to love and support you even when you're not lovable.

The what-is, pain and all, is the best thing any of us has—and realizing that is the only path to the what-will-be.

CHAPTER TWELVE

BACK FOR GOOD

One of the hardest things about my brain being sick was how different my memory became. As a kid, I had a near-photographic memory that made school easy. I was able to pull up pictures and paragraphs from books I had read. I was two grades ahead in math, advanced in English, and able to graduate a year and a half early. That's how I went to Portland State while I played with the Winterhawks during the season and I worked jobs on the side in the summer. I worked hard at school, but it was easy to do.

After all of the concussions and the damage of that final injury, I had to learn *how to learn*. This was especially difficult when I decided I needed to get my real estate license. I went to the Arizona School of Real Estate and Business, whose graduates have a 95 percent pass rate in the state test. It's a difficult program for anyone to get through, much less someone who has trouble retrieving information from their brain. There were hundreds of vocabulary words to learn, which I had to study over and over and over again in order to retain them. I would try to make up rhymes and devices to pull them up on the test. I worked for months just to figure out how I could learn, and even then, it took two tries to pass my test—which meant another round of studying in between.

I missed the 85 percent benchmark by 2 percent on the first attempt, so I retook it after some more studying and passed with flying colors the second attempt. All in spite of how difficult it had become for me to recall information. I was truly amazed and proud that I was able to figure out a way to get the job done. At the end of 2014, three years after retiring and months after dragging myself through pain and memory loss and a loss of myself to get to that Tony Robbins event, I earned my real estate license.

And I didn't really tell anyone.

Unlike my accomplishments in hockey, which were under the microscope for every win and loss and hang-up along the way, this one was just for me. The accomplishment was something much bigger than a way to negotiate real estate for my family or close friends. It was a way to make my brain turn on again. It was a challenge that I could take on even though my body wouldn't let me push it in the ways I had done for my whole life.

I wasn't going to be a real estate agent for the rest of my life. Sitting in open houses and making cold calls was not my purpose in life, and I knew that. But pushing myself beyond my injury to accomplish something that was just for me—not a coach or a crowd or a GM—did something incredible for my brain and my spirit, and I'll forever be grateful for that experience. But my true purpose was about healing.

Every morning, I reconnect with that universal energy from God, meditating and asking for that light to move through the parts of my body that need to heal. On those days, the screaming and the play and the chaos that my kids bring into the world just sound beautiful. Brooke thinks I'm tuning them out sometimes, but I'm not. I just have this observer who sees them as healthy and strong and fiery and independent. I'm not using an observer who's looking for everything they've done wrong. I'm looking at the thousand amazing coincidences that had to line up for them to exist and for me to be there with them in that moment, even if that moment is argumentative and loud.

I still connect with healers Tony introduced to me as well. One guy, Donny Epstein, can be five feet away from me and adjust my spine in a rolling wave of energy with the flick of his wrist or a gentle touch. Others offer meditation or coaching training. It's incredible to have that access to the help that I need when I need it.[28] I don't know if I'll ever be physically 100 percent again. I can work out again and can skate again at charity events or when I'm coaching my kids. If I give it 100

---

28 Someday, over a beer, ask me about the woman who orgasmed during the entire energy session Donny did with her five feet away from me. It was totally an "I'll have what she's having" moment, but for energy work. While we're at it, you might also ask me how I came to like beer after being allergic to it my entire life—when a grand master healer swished it around in his mouth and spat it back out into my glass for me to drink. Crazy, fun, amazing stuff.

percent, then I start to feel pulling sensations in my neck, or I feel slightly foggy the next morning after a max effort skate or workout, but I'm usually clear again in a day or two.

And the thing is, that's my life without any drugs. Without any injections. Without any kind of treatment other than reconnecting with God and myself on a regular basis.

///

When I finally started coaching, I tried to hang onto the definition of a coach that I grew up with—I helped a guy who was trying to get to the NHL. Then, by word of mouth, I branched out a little more and helped an entrepreneur who was going through a divorce and potential bankruptcy. As I started helping people, they told others about the results they had when they worked with me. Then others wanted to see me, hoping they could get those same results. They wanted to lose sixty-five pounds, save their marriage, have a million-dollar turnaround, or find a deeper connection to a new sense of purpose. God delivered these wins for people—I was just the delivery mechanism.

People lined up to work with me, and I was lit up with purpose and fulfillment like I hadn't been in years. I was on fire with passion for the work I was doing and the people I was doing it with. My clients became like family to me, and together we worked through things most people can't even imagine.

The more I connect with my own healing process and who I am at my core, the more comfortable I am following my instincts in a session. And sometimes outside of sessions, too.

In Tucson, Arizona, there is this place called Miraval Spa. They have all of the Tibetan sound bowls, yoga silks, and water-based healing things you'd expect at a resort, plus zip-lining, hiking, and equine therapy. And it's all just a quick getaway from our home in Phoenix.

Brooke and I went for a weekend getaway with a couple of friends of ours, and we all signed up for an equine session called "It's Not about the Horse." For that session, the staff took us and six other people—our friends, a mother and daughter pairing, and another couple who had flown in from New York—from the spa on a shuttle to someone's ranch.

As soon as the rancher walked out, Brooke started to get emotional. He looked just like her father, down to the movements and mannerisms, and her father had recently passed. The connection was immediate and eerie.

Our exercise in that session was to get the horse to lift his hoof like they do to scrape the hay and gravel out of it. It sounded simple, except the guy didn't tell us how to do it. And the horse wasn't having it.

I was the first person to try. The rancher asked me a few unrelated questions while I tried grabbing the horse's legs a little softer and then a little harder. After a couple of minutes of trying to force the horse to do what I wanted it to, I stood back for a second. Somehow, the guy managed to get me to share that I always felt like I had to take care of everyone.

As I thought about the field of energy the horse would have as another living being, the rancher said, "Well, maybe it's time you take care of yourself."

My shoulders relaxed, and the horse must have seen the real me too. There was nothing to be afraid of. He lifted his foot up for me, and we finished the exercise.

All this time, Brooke had been watching the rancher as he moved and talked. When it was her turn, he asked what was wrong. She told him it was nothing—that he reminded her of her dad who had just died a couple of months before.

"Yeah? Go on, then."

The horse immediately complied.

Not everyone in our group made it work. Some of them took twenty minutes or more to get the horse to lift its hoof for them, and the businessman who had flown in from New York couldn't get it to work at all. He was just so angry and frustrated. It was like the horse was calling us on our masks and walls. If we weren't open, we might not be safe. It was never about getting the horse to do something but about changing ourselves.

The mother, who seemed extremely timid and frail, moved slowly, limping out to the horse using her walker, but couldn't find the energy to try anything more. When the rancher tried to help the woman, she started to cry. Come to find out, she and her daughter were there because her body was filled with stage IV cancer. It was terminal, and she was preparing to die.

Now we were all crying.

Watching her struggle back to the bus with her bad knee, emotionally drained, I felt connected to her just like I had connected to that horse just a minute ago. I didn't know what I could do, but it seemed like there had to be something. I felt drawn to her. Getting off the bus, I caught her for a moment and shared that with her. I told her I had just been to India and had some interesting training around energy, and she was happy to hear about it and said she was open to me trying something out.

The villa she was staying in with her daughter was beautiful. We sat on the deck that overlooked the desert and palm trees spread out toward the base of the mountains, and she asked me what she needed to do.

"Not much, really. Just sit here and enjoy this beautiful scenery and tell me about how much you appreciate your life."

So she did. She told me about her kids and her life. While earlier she had talked about being scared to die so young, now she was telling me about all of the beautiful things in her world. Then I told her about my life too. I told her about how I died and how expansive and beautiful heaven was. I told her about the energy and love and grace and freedom and lightness that I felt. How it was soft and easy and beautiful. And as she spoke and I spoke, all of that fear and terror she held earlier seemed to melt into openness. Almost relief or excitement. I could feel her shifting.

Then I turned on some music, and we started to do some energy work. For forty-five minutes, I worked on her, and for forty-five minutes, that sense of energy grew and grew. Later, her daughter told me that these little black flies had been all over the porch, but the longer we worked, the fewer there were. They landed on her while she watched the session, but none landed on her mom or me during the entire forty-five minutes. It was like we were in this little bubble of light, love, and peace. We felt so connected that I could taste the chemicals from her treatments. By the end, when I felt like things had changed, I hugged her and told her I loved her and then went back to my room.

That night at dinner, this woman breezed into the dining room, absolutely radiant. No sunglasses, no hat covering her bald head, no limp at all, and absolutely no fear on her face. She had been so scared for so long, carrying so much pain in that knee and worry in her heart, but all of that was gone. Brooke was a little amused that I had spent so much time with these complete strangers, but the joy on both of their faces was unmistakable, and it was so real and beautiful.

Maybe that was her only day that was pain-free, or maybe she was comfortable for the rest of her life. Maybe her stage IV cancer went away, though it probably didn't. As we were getting ready to leave our hotel room, I saw that they had left a beautifully wrapped package sitting in front of my hotel room door. It was a book about angels, and inside the book were all these beautiful quotations and notes from both the mom and daughter. They said how grateful they were for our time together, that they believed angels do live on earth, and they believed I was one of them.

Tears welled in my eyes as I read through the book and all of the amazing things they had written inside of it. I said a little prayer for the family and for the mom, that she'd fully recover and live a vibrant life. Or, if it was her time to go, that she'd go with little to no pain, and she'd experience all of God and heaven unencumbered with pure love, joy, and bliss. I never heard from them again to know. What I do believe, with everything in my heart, is that her journey to the other side was a celebration.

My job was to build a bridge. It was to fulfill my promise from years before that I would carry what I experienced in that brief moment of death back to as many people as I could. That's the promise that I made to God, and it comes with a whole lot of vulnerability.

I used to worry that people would think I'm crazy, but time after time and miracle after miracle, they don't. They begin to believe because they can see the truth in me and the results in them.

Every coaching client who has come to me has brought some kind of story with them, some kind of negative perception that became the foundation of their armor that we have had to work to peel back, bit by bit. When I see that glow that comes from the healing that energy like that brings, none of that matters. Because it's not about me anyway. The change they experience is real. I can see their energy shift and change from the start of the call or session to the end of it in popping necks and backs · aligning, in big deep breaths and signs of relief.

I can feel their lives change in every cell of my body. I watch as the generations of trauma and pain and protection that they carry with them—and we all carry that with us—get disrupted with a new way of thinking. With a new way of being. And I know in every ounce of my being that they're going to be okay.

///

The term *life coach* is so overused now. A lot of people pretend to be coaches but have no idea what they're actually doing. It takes a special person, or a person with very special experiences, to be able to deal with the different personalities and problems that come into a coaching space—to understand someone else's model of the world, background, culture, and belief systems and not have any judgment or preconceived notions. I realized my own experiences and training were about more than just hockey.[29] I can't really pigeonhole my work when there are people out there who need me. This is serious stuff. It's not something to dabble in. If I had to pick a niche, I wanted it to just be people. I didn't care if I was working with professional athletes or poker players or lawyers or stay-at-home moms or celebrities.

I want to believe in people like my dad believed in me. I want them to trust me like I trusted him.

There was no one else I could really tell the truth about who I was and how I was feeling. I could tell my dad when I was really hurt. I could tell him and my mom when I was heartbroken about losing Adam and Nicholas to cancer. Dad had this incredible way of acknowledging the pain and reframing it for me so that I could keep going. My mom was supportive, but she didn't know what to say. I love my wife so much, but sometimes she didn't know what to say either. My teammates didn't want to look vulnerable either, so they didn't have a lot to say. We supported each other, but compassion was kind of a rare thing. Being injured or in pain was just part of the job.

I got a glimpse of that trust when I was on pause working for the NHL Players Association after my fourth concussion wouldn't allow me to play. A player called me to tell me he got rocked in a couple of fights and was sure he had a concussion. He couldn't see really well and was worried about the next game. With the toughest guy in the league on the other

---

29 I recently learned that my great-grandmother on my mother's side, who I never met, was a healer back in Ukraine that people would come from all over to see. Maybe more of her is in me than I knew.

team, he was worried that a fight could literally kill him. And he couldn't tell his team, or they would find an excuse to send him down.

I actually called the tough guy on the other team personally and told him the situation. I asked him to give him a pass and let him take a few more days to heal up. The player absolutely understood, and everyone is still alive.

Who knows what could have happened without that phone call. But the fact that it took a third party to make that happen is a problem. He was too afraid to tell the truth because he could lose his entire career. But he could tell me, and I could do something to help save his life. That's how I want to coach people.

That's how I want to parent.

All three of my kids are such funny little people. They have the best senses of humor and are always teasing each other. They're strong kids with their own personalities.

When she was little, Olivia called herself the O-meister. She knew it all from the very beginning, and she'd tell you about it in a tiny little Smurf voice. She's thirteen now, and so talented at everything that she does. She's athletic and strong and picks up stuff so quickly. But more importantly, she's got a good head on her shoulders. She's responsible, caring, and wiser than her years. It's like she's been around the block already—one of the smartest kids I've ever met. I'm so excited to see how her future unfolds.

My second-born, Caden, is a gentle, sensitive soul who has special powers that he doesn't quite realize yet. Watching him today, I think he has some of that photographic memory that I had when I was little too. He comprehends everything that he reads, and I bet he reads a hundred books a year—at least five times through the Harry Potter series already, probably more by the time this book is finished. He used to want to be an inventor. I can't wait to see what he'll be.

My youngest, Sawyer, is the biggest ham—a jokester who's always making people laugh. He's such a thinker about God and life and people. He's our little cuddler, so in tune with people and animals. He's still experimenting with everything to see what he really enjoys. This is his first year of hockey, and he played football this year too. Sawyer is still little, but I see that fire in him to stand up for people around him. He's protected friends against bullies and is always watching to be sure we're fair when his siblings get in trouble. He'll defend the people he loves no matter what.

It's incredible to see that they all have such different personalities and talents, but they all have little pieces of me too. They're my greatest achievement.

Sometimes I watch for glimmers of the obsessive drive that I had as a kid. Olivia has some of the competitiveness that I used to have—she gets angry if she loses, and that's something that's in her. It's not taught. But she hasn't channeled any of that energy into a sport yet. She's naturally gifted enough that her PE teacher told us to put her in track. But she's just not interested in doing it all the time.

Caden sets goals like I did. He made himself a promise that he would learn how to do a backflip on the trampoline within two weeks of learning how to do a front flip. It was something that made him uncomfortable and scared him a little, but he went after it anyway. When he finally nailed it, the joy in him was like a fire. Then he was out there doing backflips every night, which escalated to backflips standing on the ground. Caden now flips off of structures, benches, picnic tables, boats, everything. He side flips, front flips, and backflips, and yesterday he told me he is going to master a double backflip on the trampoline.

Today, we're running them to sports on Tuesdays, Wednesdays, Thursdays, Saturdays, and Sundays, and I coach them in both hockey and baseball. Just like my dad let me choose my path, I am here for my kids whether they want to be athletes, inventors, architects, herpetologists, or garbage collectors.

As long as they love their lives, I'll love them with them. I teach them to be fulfilled and to be challenged so that they are happy but also progressing and growing. If life gets too easy, the energy stops flowing. It doesn't matter to me what they do as long as they're engaged in it every minute.

As long as they know that they are so loved and that they can love others just as fully. Brooke and I have shared affection with them that my dad sometimes struggled with and that his dad could never offer. We're open and honest about times that we've been scared or worried or picked on or stressed out. We make sure they are comfortable enough to talk about those things too. We talk about how it's okay to be scared and do it anyway. We talk about how you never fail; you only learn. We're trying to help them change those negative thought patterns before they get a chance to become their normal way of thinking.

It's daunting. Am I doing enough? Have I done too much? We're only really given eighteen summers with our kids. I've got just a few more with my daughter. So what am I doing with that time? What am I giving her now that will support the rest of her journey?

That's the kind of coach I want to be. One who's there for their whole life—as it is, not as we'd like it to be—loving them, supporting them, and pushing them to be more present and engaged in whatever they're after.

I give everything I have to my clients, just like I laid everything out on the ice when I was playing. At the end of the day, I get that same rush of productive exhaustion that you get after training really hard. My muscles are exhausted; my brain has been stretched, and I lie in bed thanking God for the opportunity to be the middleman for that level of healing for people.

///

I used to think life was all about setting goals. I thought I could go for an exact number of points and assists and then raise the bar every year. That works out as a young kid when everyone gets equal time on the ice, but eventually, you start to lose control. If your groin tweaks or your arm breaks or a coach doesn't like you enough to give you time, there's not much you can do about it. For years, I kept trying. I set goals and pushed myself and then was hard on myself when I didn't get there.

It wasn't until I did an interview with Sean Burke years later when we created the *Hockey Star Secrets* documentary that I realized it's not about the outcome at all. He told me, "I want to look in the mirror every day and be able to say I gave everything that I had."

That's something I can control.

I can leave it all on the ice. I can practice with focus and passion. I can give my clients everything I've got. I can take care of that vulnerable part of myself with meditation and focus. I can spend time with my family and be present in every moment.

Some of my best times weren't when a goal was met but when I got to be with my guys—especially my roommates. Those dudes saw more of me than anyone else. They were the closest thing I had to a place to be safe and vulnerable because we were all there together, living out our dreams and trying to figure out what that meant. We could rant to each other, complain, support each other, and understand each other.

After the last concussion, it was the first time in thirty years that I hadn't been part of a team. With the different coaching groups and mastermind groups that I joined, they became a new sort of team, with shared experiences that no one else would understand. More recently, I've built my own community around my coaching clients. But there was something special about those teammates that was incredibly hard to lose.

Guys on teams like the Detroit Redwings formed a close family who stayed together year after year. Guys like me who played on rebuilding teams wound up with new people all the time. I have hundreds of brothers out there, and I genuinely care about all of them. They're still family. We sacrificed our time and our bodies and our energy. We all had each other's backs and experienced this crazy life together.

Today, I might get a text from Mattias, telling me he saw some old pictures or just that he thought about me. Or we'll pick up and play golf after years, and it'll be like we never missed a beat. And every year, now that I'm healthy again, the Coyote alumni get together and play against the college kids like Arizona State or Northern Arizona University. Those kids can fly, but they don't have the experience that we have. They don't know how to be in the right place making the right move like we do, and we beat them every time. Our record is something like 149-1.

Whenever we play that game against NAU, we always stay there overnight. Afterward, we go over to these college kids' dorms or fraternity houses to play beer pong and tell stories like we'd been to war together. And in some ways, we had.

For my group of buddies especially, most of us shouldn't have made it at all. To play the game we loved and get paid for it, to make it out from nothing and live this crazy, amazing life together...there's something really special about it that you can only understand if you've lived it.

Many of us are lucky to have lived to tell about it at all. So many of our teammates and fellow athletes across other sports have gone from rock stars with the world at their fingertips to trying to escape the world because their brains betrayed them. Because their organizations failed them.

As of right now, the NHL hasn't admitted that CTE and damage from concussions are a byproduct of the game. After players retire, they stop all significant medical coverage, leaving people like me paying $30,000 a year for insurance. Former Stanley Cup winners are living in tents and under bridges because they gave everything they had to give and then were left out in the cold.

I think of what Shane Doan said when he spoke at our trainer Jukka Nieminen's funeral.[30] He said, "People think these guys are just our trainers, but our trainers are part of our team. We spend more time during the season with our teams than we do with our wives or kids."

For years, we were family. I could fill a whole set of books with our stories. With everything that I learned from my teammates and coaches and trainers and experiences. You've got this window of a decade, if you're lucky, to play in the best league in the world. For most guys, it's half of that or less. In that time, your life is going to change forever. Unfortunately, the organizations that bring teams together like this—especially when you're likely to be injured or experience trauma—don't always have your back. But we've got each other, and we've got our stories. Eventually, hopefully, that will lead to change. Other professional sports leagues cover players' medical insurance after they retire, and others set aside substantial amounts of money for players for post-career treatments and surgery. Hopefully, that will one day happen for the players in the National Hockey League.[31]

As far as my career and my journey go, I wouldn't change any of it for anything. Would I try to celebrate my wins more and stand up for myself when I needed to? Sure, but everything

---

30 Shane was the team captain of the Coyotes, and Jukka Nieminen passed away the night before his wedding. His fiancé actually wore her wedding dress to the funeral. We were all heartbroken to lose him.

31 I know the NHL Alumni Association has brought up this topic for discussion, and I am praying for future and existing alumni that this will become a reality. There are lots of guys out there who need it.

that happened was a lesson. Even the biggest injury allowed me to close a door that I couldn't close on my own.

Something huge had to happen to end that stage of my life. I wasn't going to make that change on my own. I couldn't go the places I was meant to go by being the person I was before.

Everything has been by design. All the good, all the bad, all the ups, all the downs. All perfectly designed to bring me here, to this moment, with these words on this page. It was all leading me to now.

*At five years old, the most authentic, pure version of my soul.
This photo means more to me than anyone will ever know.*

*Me and Tony Robbins at his Sun Valley home around 2013. Fun fact:
there's a hot spring in his home that the Dalai Lama once came to visit.*

Sage Robbins giving me a Deeksha blessing at the Oneness Temple in Chennai, India.

Me and Tony as he tried to do an intervention about my things that made me angry in other people—but I was too blissed out to come up with an answer. Hilarious moment also in India.

*Caesars, cigars, and backgammon with my dad. The cigars were
a rare treat, but backgammon was a ruthless tradition. We played
countless games for nickels and dimes out at the lake every summer.*

*The whole squad—parents and siblings and our kids—out
on the lake one last time before my dad passed.*

*No matter how far I went or how many games I played,
I always looked forward to coming back to Salmon
Arm, BC, for time on the lake with my family.*

Family photo at the beautiful Flora Farms in Cabo, 2020.

I can't tell you how many hours I spent on the lake with my dad over the years. Seeing him here and going back to the lake always makes me miss him that much more.

I'm so blessed to have such an incredible family squad.
(Photo by Carrie Reiser, 2019)

CONCLUSION

It took me a long time to write this book. Not only to sort everything out, but to allow myself to tell it. Writing gave me permission to share, and just before I finished drafting, it happened.
I hadn't planned to tell my whole story—it was a small event
with about fifty-five financial professionals expecting to hear
about my hockey career. They sat there with arms crossed,
half engaged while this drop-in speaker they'd barely heard of
talked about sports and fighting and goals and fans and money.

With about seventeen minutes to go, the fame side of my
story started to taper off. I was stuck. There was nothing more
to say except the truth. So I leaned in.

I dug into the pain, and I took a deep breath and told them
about my near-death experience. I told them how I had died.

The room was absolutely silent, and I let the silence sit. I paused for so long, not wanting to do the experience a disservice.

I probably didn't do it justice. How can you effectively convey something that there are no words for? Every time I try, it comes out a little bit different, another piece of the most vibrant experience of my life.

As I shared the story that I thought people would judge me for, something incredible happened. I became a middleman for the message they each needed to hear. People started crying or squirming in their seats, hoping to hide. I felt connections to each of them, pulled to lock eyes with someone new in each piece of my story when it was something they needed to hear.

I never got lost or confused. It felt like I had tapped into a data center of stories and information meant for other people to hear. I've been training for this my whole life—I just had to let myself access it again.

The armor that got me through pain, through trauma, through grief and violence and death wasn't meant to hide me away. It's meant to protect—to help move me forward toward my purpose. And it's only by taking it off and becoming vulnerable again that I can finally live that purpose.

///

There is a balance to find between protection and vulnerability. Between avoidance and charging forward. If the check-engine light on your car comes on, you know the car has to be looked at. You don't leave it running for a month and then get surprised when it all breaks down. The light as warning you all along.

The more in tune I am with the light in me—that sense of little David, still pure and safe and loving—the more it becomes a warning sign or a reminder. Vulnerability allows the sensors and antennas in my energetic field to be amplified. I have learned to see, feel, and hear nudges and understand the information that God and the universe is trying to communicate with me. Guide me, warn me, alert me to help direct me quickly and safely to the right path, the right choice, the necessary action to take. Then the ripple effect that surges through the light becomes a warning—a message telling me to check in with myself to make an adjustment.

Most people in the world get these messages hundreds of times without ever knowing it because they keep layering on so much armor that they can't see that warning light anymore.

It happens to pro athletes giving up their bodies to hopefully keep their spot on the team. It happens to military service members pressing through physical extremes to complete the mission and then burying their emotional extremes to survive the trauma. It happens to first responders who have seen terrible things and parents who have carried their children through the unimaginable.

I'm not sure I could have done what I did without some level of armor. It gives you courage and strength. It makes you fearless. It keeps you disciplined and focused. All of those are great qualities. But when we forget how to take that armor off, check in with ourselves, and return to a state of vulnerability and authenticity, eventually we get disconnected from our greatest gifts. We create something else that can survive it so that our true selves don't have to be exposed to the pain.

When we get disconnected from our inner child, our authentic soul, we wind up lost. When we're no longer an NHL player, a soldier, a fireman, a stay-at-home mom, married to the person we thought we'd be with forever...what's left? Where do we go to connect with ourselves again?

I think that's why I had to die before the message sank in. If everything had been rosy, I would have kept burying my true self under so much armor that I never would have felt anything again.

When I finally made that connection again, my career changed. My life changed. My heart changed. As long as I stay tuned into those messages and stay vulnerable enough to hear them, the path that I'm on is going to continue changing lives. One of the greatest gifts I can give as a coach now is to reintroduce people to their best selves. To find the inner champion and not just the exterior gladiator. I can see the change happen in their eyes, like when a neural pathway reconnects.

If I were to go back and play today, knowing what I know now and practicing what I practice now, I wouldn't try to eliminate the gladiator and all of his armor. I would use that strength for practicing and preparing and playing games. But I would take it off enough to enjoy life more. I wouldn't stay on edge as much. I would let things go. I would explore and party and soak in the amazing time I had in the incredible career I built.

But there's no energy in living in the past. If I hadn't pushed myself so hard and hadn't broken myself so much, I wouldn't be who I am today.

There's a topography to our lives, and sometimes it does include hard mountains and dark valleys. There's no point in beating ourselves up over them. The big picture makes it clear: bad things happen, but they lead to amazing things when we're open to it.

I've got a friend who is an incredible music producer who works nonstop without vacations or breaks or anything. A little bit of that reminded me of how many shots I'd take in the backyard. I felt compelled to work hard not just so I could get better, but also because I loved it. That seems to be a common factor for a lot of the elite professions in this world. Artists and athletes and creative types who work nonstop are more likely to hyperfocus than amateurs. Even within other fields, specialization earns more than generalization. Putting in the time does bring rewards. When you're unwilling to settle where others do, you stand out.

When I asked him whether he loved that lifestyle—whether it's fulfilling to work that much—he told me something profound. He said, "Honestly, there's something broken in me. I don't want anyone to think that I got lucky or that my hits were a fluke." So he works as hard as he possibly can so that his risk of failure feels lower. So that he feels like he's earning his place in this world.

The thing is, I didn't ask him to stop. There's no reason to stop being who you are built to be. I don't think it's something broken at all. I simply suggested celebrating each win.

Whether it was a night off after a small goal or a vacation after something big happened, he needed to let himself see and celebrate his success rather than powering forward based on fear.

The answer isn't to put away the gladiator or to never fight. It's not to go off to become a monk or to show every single feeling. It's not to become something we're not. It's to be who we were meant to be from the beginning.

///

Once, while relaxing at the pool, I struck up a conversation with a woman who shared that her father had just passed. When I allowed myself to share my experience with her, the worry and pain she'd felt around his death melted away. She could relax and trust that he was in that perfect place of love and light, when even her church had given her doubts.

I wasn't really surprised that it felt new to her. I've sat in churches before, listening to preachers talk about how the people just aren't getting the message. When I look around to see all of the armor and masks the people next to me are wearing, how could any message of love do anything but bounce right off? Nothing can get to our hearts and our souls when we're so covered up. When we're afraid to be vulnerable and exposed. And that's not surprising either. We're bombarded with messages from each other, from media, from the internet, from our peers, from our careers—all telling us how we need to be. Not to mention the churches that give us rules instead of grace and judgment instead of love.

That's not the God that I experienced.

The God that I met was nothing but love and grace. That belief doesn't come with unbreakable rules and stress and guilt. It comes with power and energy and love and trust and balance. And until we all learn to take off the armor and the masks and the layers that have protected us for so long, the message will keep bouncing off of those walls.

Even when we don't feel like it, we're always being taken care of. If you're stuck, there's an answer sitting right beside you. But you're not going to get to it by walking in the same circle, staying in the same box. You have to expand. Become open and resourceful enough to access it.

It doesn't take a blow to the head to get me to listen anymore, thankfully. If God nudges me, I try to listen, even if I don't know where we're going with it. It feels like I've lived five lives already with everything that happened to me. And every time I let everything else go and just follow my instincts, I'm blessed in return.

We're taught to soften everything, to gloss over the hard things and the weird things and the painful things—the things that are difficult to believe and difficult to express. But that's not where healing lives. My joy came when I stopped protecting myself, stopped shielding and hiding my heart and my soul. When I ripped off all the armor and said, "Here I am! This is me. Love me or hate me." When I decided I was never following anyone but this pure little angel child inside of me. When I realized I don't have to fight anymore.

I believe I'm able to coach well because I can give people the resources to access that next level. To shift into another perspective, another way of operating. When we go into that space, it's like magic. Bodies heal, and cancer is stripped of its fear. We start to believe in the magic we believed in as kids.

So much can happen on your journey, whether it's to the NHL or to overcome trauma or just to find yourself again. The people making the biggest impact are the people who are truly in love with the truth. They're just real. They play the game differently. They stop limiting themselves.

I couldn't get healing until I found little David again, and you won't be able to, either, until you find allow yourself to heal your body and soul openly and completely. Reconnecting to your inner, authentic self is essential in expanding to that next level. The child is creativity and joy and play, and the champion is passion and drive and work. The more you can bring those pieces of yourself together, the better you'll be able to come back from life's blows.

That's what this world was created for. That's the message I'm here to share. Thank you for listening to my story. I look forward to our paths crossing again soon.

Author's note: It's not an accident that this book is in your hands right now. If you're feeling buried under your own rubble of armor, masks, and years of protective layers, please know that there is beautiful life on the other side. I'd love to be the guy who can help you become your authentic self, make changes in your life, and return to vulnerability and joy. For all the ways you can connect and work with me, visit Comeback.DaveScatchard.com. I would so love to hear from you.

ACKNOWLEDGMENTS

I would like to first and foremost thank God for our meeting together and for all of the incredible blessings that you have bestowed upon me and my family. Being filled with the faith that you always have my back and that you are always guiding me has allowed me to live a joyous and burdenless life, and I am so grateful for that and for you allowing me to spend time on the other side with you.

To my amazing mom, you have always been the nurturer, the source of love, comfort, and a safe place for me to go over all the craziness of my journey. You are loving but still strong. You have always supported me and our family with unconditional love. I wouldn't be the man I am today or have reached any of my dreams if you had not been supporting me every step of the way, all while raising two other great kids at the same time.

Heather, thank you for always supporting me, and I don't know how I can ever replace all those Dad hours that I borrowed from you and Doug while he was driving me around the country playing hockey and chasing my dreams! You are an amazing wife and mom to Troy, Ridge, and Lilliana.

To my little bro, Doug! I am so lucky that you are my brother—to have someone who is cool and fun and just loves to love life is such a gift. Your big smile and terrible jokes always make me laugh. You were and continue to be a bright light of love and laughter in our family. Your sense of humor and your laid-back attitude really are so easy to be around. Thank you for being one of my biggest fans and supporters my whole life. You are a great dad, and I can't wait to hang out with you and your beautiful, growing family more.

Brooke, my amazing, incredible, loving wife. Since the first day I laid eyes on you, I have known that you and I were meant to spend our lives together. Your selflessness and skill to put our kids and me and my dreams ahead of your own is something I can never repay. I thank God every day that he brought you into my life because you make me a better man just by being around you. Thank you for all you do for me and our family.

Olivia, you are such a special soul. You can be incredible at anything you want to in life. You have internal drive, hunger, and passion, and that is so fun for me to watch as your dad. You are wise beyond your years, and you are a leader; use that gift for good as you move forward in your life. You can change the world if you want to. I love you to the moon and back forever.

Caden, you are one of the most pure, kind souls I have ever seen. You have gifts that you are just starting to tap into now that will allow you to see things in life that no one else does. I pray that you refine these gifts to light up this world with your purity and innocence.

Sawyer, you are one of the funniest, coolest kids I know. Your sense of humor always makes everyone laugh, but my favorite part of you is your willingness to stick up for people and what you believe to be right. I feel that you have special gifts as well that are beyond what we can see, and I am looking forward to you realizing these gifts and using them for good in this world. Keep praying and talking to God—he will always be listening.

Grandma B, thank you for always being loving and supportive. Your hugs and grandma cookies and pierogies were always my favorite, and the strength you carried with you from a young girl leaving home at an early age to seek a better life has been transferred down the line for generations. I know that you passed that strength down to me, and I am truly grateful for that, and for all of the magic moments we get together—especially our epic Scrabble battles at the cabin. I love you Grandma.

To Glenda, Bryan, Brett, Brandon, and Kara. Thank you for sharing your daughter/sister with me and raising such an amazing soul. You all are so fun, and I love each and every one of you and every time we get the families together. Thank you for loving my family like it's yours.

For my first life, I would like to thank all of the GMs and coaches who drafted me and signed me and ultimately believed in me, and who trusted that I could help their teams win by having me on them.

My roommates Mattias Ohlund, Peter Schaefer, Brad Isbister. I'm so glad we got to enjoy each other's company and chase our dreams together. You guys are like brothers to me, and I will never forget our crazy adventures together.

To every teammate I have ever played with at any level of hockey. We are forever brothers and bonded in ways most people won't ever understand. Going to war with someone and spending most of the hours of most of your days striving to win and achieve greatness while competing at world-class levels is special. Very few will ever get to experience anything close to that in their entire lives, and I am grateful that I got to have those magic moments with all of you.

To all of my childhood friends who have cheered me on my entire career and always had my back. Todd Scott (ORS), my undercover bodyguard, thank you for always watching my back. Jason Potter, one of my oldest friends—we started hockey together. Our dads worked in the mines together, and you have known me longer than anyone. Sorry for shooting a tennis ball through your mom's window when we were eight—my aim was a little off back then. Holtsey and Mueller, Connor, Borsato, and all the Salmon Arm boys, thanks for always cheering me on and supporting me. Winning provincials with you all was one of the highlights of my hockey career. Thanks for the great memories and laughs. Thanks to all my Hinton buddies who traveled around Alberta with me, taking on anyone who would play us.

To every medical trainer I have had in my career, thank you for keeping me in the lineup, taping me back together, and finding a way to help me play through the pain on an almost nightly basis.

To every strength coach I have had during my journey, thank you for pushing me, guiding me, and building my body and mind into a world-class athlete. I will always be grateful.

For my second life, I would like to thank all of the doctors, chiropractors, acupuncturists, and massage therapists I have worked with over the last decade to get better.

Tony Robbins, thank you for being an inspiration and mentor to me. Thank you for dragging my ass around the world to learn, grow, and expand, while introducing me to an entirely different world that in my heart I knew existed but had trouble seeing. The guides, philosophies, and people you introduced me to are now staples in my life. Thank you for showing me what is possible and reminding me that a wizard can do more in his pinkie than a gladiator can do in his lifetime.

Donny Epstein, I just want you to know that when I first started working with you, I was like, "Holy shit, this guy gets it!" You are at another level. I also felt like you could put words and structure to the things that I know to be true about God, the universe, and the soul. We are brothers for this lifetime and beyond! I look forward to more adventures soon.

Dr. Barry Morguelan, you are a special person with special gifts. Keep using them for good. Thank you for your magical healings of my broken bones in my hands twice! Thank you for what you are doing in this world.

To all of my All-Star Coaching 1x1 clients, my All-Star mastermind, and group coaching clients. Thank you for playing full out.

To the tens of thousands of others who have gone through the Get Your Life Together Challenge. Thank you for your belief in me to help get you next-level results. Thank you for your willingness to do some of the crazy things that I say. Stay open-minded to the magic of creating a greater win-win-win relationship for all of humanity. I love you all and will always be there for you. Looking forward to working together and creating many more adventures together soon!

Thank you to the NHL for providing the greatest memories of my life and such an incredible league to play in.

Thank you to all my friends over at the NHLPA and the NHL Alumni offices for supporting me and the other players during our careers and now after with the alumni stuff.

Eric Lindros, thank you for hiring me to work for the NHLPA before my comeback. The love you have for your fellow NHLPA members and standing up for them was inspiring and powerful; not only were you one of the best to ever play the game, but I am grateful to have gotten to know you while working with you at the PA as opposed to trying to slow you down playing against you for all those years.

I would also like to thank Wayne McBean, Greg Adams, and the rest of my buddies on the Coyote alumni team for giving me a safe place to land and to find that fellowship and brotherhood that I was missing in my life. So far, we have raised over $1.4 million for various charities, and it has been a blast doing it alongside you. Thanks for giving me a place to go that feels like a team and allowing me to get back on the ice safely and have a blast playing hockey again.

To Chief and the Nickelback boys, thank you for always taking such good care of me, my family, and my teammates. Always fun times, laughs, and magic memories. Love you guys.

To Brannan, thank you so much for your patience and input on how to bring all these stories together, giving my voice some framework and structure but keeping the authenticity of it. You're the best, and I am truly grateful.

To the entire publishing team at Scribe, thank you for helping me put the pieces together for this book. There are so many moving pieces, and I couldn't have done it without you. Many more to come!

Please know that if I did not name you, it doesn't mean that you didn't have a major impact in my life. I don't think there are enough trees to make enough paper for me to thank everyone I want to.

ABOUT THE AUTHOR

Dave Scatchard had a fourteen-year career as a hockey player in the NHL, but after his fifth concussion left him with slurred speech, headaches, and traumatic brain injuries, he embarked on a journey around the world to restore his health and reinvent his life.

With the guidance of top coaches, healers, and energy workers, Dave transformed himself and developed a systematic coaching approach for both businesses and individuals to redesign their outlook and envision a healthier, brighter future.

Dave lives in Arizona with his wife, three kids, and two dogs. For more information, visit *ComeBack.DaveScatchard.com.*